GETTING STARTED AS A FREELANCE ILLUSTRATOR OR DESIGNER

ACKNOWLEDGMENTS

I am indebted to the following friends and colleagues for their generous help, expert advice and words of wisdom: Nick Albright, Bob Bingenheimer, Ms. Pat Campbell, Carol Buchanan, Gerald H. Grayson, Dan Johnson, Debbie Kokoruda, Art Krummel, Ingrid Hansen-Lynch, Steve Miller, Bil Myers, Ms. Marty Roelandt, Ms. Theo Stephan, Kim Thompson and all the babysitters, Kim Muller-Thym, Carole Winters, Mike Woolley, and Kim Zarley.

The author wishes to express a special thanks to Susan Conner, without whom *Getting Started* could not have started at all.

ABOUT THE AUTHOR

Michael Fleishman is a freelance illustrator whose work appears in advertising, newspapers and publications (from *Orange Coast Magazine* to *Delaware Today*), children's books and educational materials (The Trumpet Club, Harper & Row, Thomas Nelson), and greeting cards for folks like Oatmeal Studios and Argus Communications. He draws the line at his studio in Yellow Springs, Ohio, around his cat Lucy (who's sleeping on the light table at this very moment).

GETTING STARTED AS A
FREELANCE
ILLUSTRATOR
OR DESIGNER

Michael   Fleishman

NORTH
LIGHT
BOOKS Cincinnati, Ohio

Getting Started as a Freelance Illustrator or Designer Copyright ©
1990 by Michael C. Fleishman. Printed and bound in United States of
America. All rights reserved. No part of this book may be reproduced in
any form or by any electronic or mechanical means including information storage and retrieval systems without permission in writing from
the publisher, except by a reviewer, who may quote brief passages in a
review. Published by North Light Books, an imprint of F&W Publications, Inc., 1507 Dana Avenue, Cincinnati, Ohio, 45207. First edition.

94 93 92 91   5 4 3 2

Library of Congress Cataloging in Publication Data

Fleishman, Michael C.
    Getting started as a freelance illustrator or designer / Michael C.
Fleishman.
        p.   cm.
    ISBN 0-89134-331-8
    1. Magazine illustration—United States—Marketing. 2. Design ser-
vices—United States—Marketing. 3. Self-employed—United States—
Employment.   I. Title.
NC968.F54 1990   89-26541
741.6′068′8—dc20   CIP

Cover illustration by Michael C. Fleishman.
© 1989 Michael C. Fleishman.

For JoJo Beany-Head,
Jack Cooper, Normie
and
Gramma Dee

CONTENTS

INTRODUCTION

I remember those first efforts very clearly. It occurred to me that freelance illustration would be a fun way to put my art to work. I bought the biggest portfolio I could find, loaded it with the best of my graduate material and, setting my sights high, dropped my portfolio off at a most prestigious greeting card company (which shall remain nameless).

At the time, my pen-and-ink drawings were hardly light and whimsical, but I figured—hey, they'll be able to see I can draw, right? Not only was my portfolio rejected, but it was returned with bits of somebody's lunch and manicure statically charged to the acetate. Talk about dejection!

But I believed in that portfolio. With some evaluation and a bit of regrouping, my next stop brought me two immediate assignments for a local newspaper. It was a great kick, opening the Sunday edition at the laundromat and seeing my illustrations in print. I was freelancing, and I was hooked.

Landing your first assignment is probably the biggest stumbling block in a career. There are no set rules. Unfortunately, we usually learn the business by making many mistakes, which is very discouraging.

Presented in a question-and-answer format, *Getting Started as a Freelance Illustrator or Designer* addresses the common problems facing those who want to freelance. We want to save the beginner some painful lessons by answering basic questions about:

- How to find jobs in your own backyard.
- How to analyze what market is right for you.
- Ways to beat the competition in picking up new business.
- How to get noticed.
- What art directors want to see.
- How to network, get referrals—and more!

Interviews with artists—both "big guns" and "young turks"—highlight how these illustrators got their foot in the door, their trials and tribulations in starting out, and their advice to the novice. Our illustrators discuss how they got their first assignments, explain how they made initial contacts, what was sent in that early package and how they followed through.

Look for special sidebars such as "Seven Laws of Submitting Work Through the Mail," "Fifteen Quick and Easy Ways to Lose Clients," and "The Ten Commandments of Freelancing" to get a well-rounded perspective from men and women who've been there.

Maybe you're a beginning illustrator, designer, or cartoonist who wants to freelance but doesn't know where to start. Perhaps you're just getting out of art school and want to market your skills. You could be a staff artist, interested in branching off, or a fine artist wanting to explore graphic art markets. Wherever you are on the ladder, we're going to present a positive yet truthful look at freelancing. So, how do you get that first assignment? Read on!

—Michael Fleishman

CHAPTER 1
WHY SHOULD YOU FREELANCE?

DEFINING FREELANCING

Q. *What is a freelancer?*

A. Defined simply, a freelancer is a self-employed subcontractor who markets his or her art by the job to several buyers. That's very short and sounds just as sweet. In the real world, and beyond the dictionary, a freelancer is also the office manager, secretarial pool, sales staff, marketing department, maintenance and mail room staff rolled into one. The ever-growing stack labeled "Important Things That Must Be Done Right Now" lies immediately under the bowling ball, cleaver, and cream pie you'll swear you're juggling as a one-person shop.

Common to all freelancers (in fact, their primary motivation) is a dedicated passion for their chosen vocation. It's more than a mere job — it's a calling. A freelancer is an entrepreneur with an independent spirit, a sense of adventure, and a bold, personal vision of success. A freelancer doesn't want to work for somebody else; there is a certain pride you get only from working for yourself. A freelance business is the vehicle for exercising your particular talents as your own boss, in your environment of choice, at the hours you choose.

ADVANTAGES AND DISADVANTAGES OF FREELANCING

Q. *What are the pluses and minuses of freelancing?*

A. The pluses offset the minuses, so I'll list them together:

■ The buzzword here is "more." As a freelance illustrator you can do a wider variety of more creative assignments, do more of the type of work you want to do, with the potential to earn more money in the process.

■ Freelancing is a demanding vocation. You're going to hustle. You'll work extended hours, but it's your schedule.

■ Freedom, at last. Providing you meet your deadlines, you decide when you go to work, and for how long. No toiling "nine-to-five" (and no time clock to punch), unless you want it that way.

■ Say a fond good-bye to that grumpy manager staring over your shoulder. Look in the mirror and meet a tough new employer. A freelancer must have great reserves of self-discipline; if you don't, you won't be working this time next year.

■ The steady paycheck is history. Your money will come in dribbles, drabs, spurts, and bursts. You will finally understand the true meaning of the terms "accounts receivable" and "accounts payable." Boys and girls, can you say "Cash flow"?

■ What you knew as professional security in your full-time position is not applicable here, as freelancing can be a bit of an emotional and fiscal roller coaster ride. Jobs may not be steady; you may miss a meal or two. You won't land every exciting assignment you pursue, and you'll have to take some mundane jobs simply to pay the bills.

■ Many people actually believe that because you freelance from home, you're not really working. As your business takes off, you'll be working alone, without the feedback and camaraderie of co-workers, weathering the peaks and valleys minus the support system of an office or staff.

■ That salesman's position your dad was always telling you about? Congratulations, you got the job! Marketing and self-promotion will become very important to you. Like it or not, we should emphasize right now that this is a business. However, the worlds of art and commerce can be quite compatible — how else could there be so many successful illustrators out there?

■ Good organization skills will be crucial. While it is the art that'll be your bread and butter, realize early that an artist's beret is only one hat you'll be wearing. Remember your co-workers at Chaingang, Slavemine, and Sweatshop? All those people, doing all those things. Working all day. Getting it all done. Those are all your responsibilities now.

■ Understand that the competition is awesome, in numbers and ability. But you're up to the challenge, right? Your new boss thinks so.

■ Come April 15, you'll benefit from the same tax breaks any small business enjoys.

■ Drawing must be your love—something enjoyed with all your heart, something you need to do, something you would do purely for yourself without pay. When you come right down to it, how many folks can say they truly love their work? As a freelance illustrator, you can—and that's the biggest plus of all.

QUALIFICATIONS FOR FREELANCING

Q. *How do I find out if I have the right stuff for freelancing?*

A. If you bought this book, you have more than a vague curiosity about going out on your own. That's a good sign right there. You won't be required to break the sound barrier every workday, but ask yourself these questions:

■ What are you getting out of this? Why are you doing it? Question your motives and answer honestly. You can make a nice chunk of change freelancing, but you could also win the lottery before you create the next Garfield. If you want to freelance just for some easy "big bucks," you're in for a rude surprise.

■ Do you have a special skill that translates into a moneymaking opportunity? Your business exists only to profitably practice your craft. Without talent, this framework—no matter how structured—won't take you very far.

■ Do you have the drive and ambition to turn that skill into a success? Talent without drive and motivation does not generate income. A dream without desire cannot be fulfilled. Freelancing should be what you *have* to do—for your soul and your checkbook.

■ How's your business acumen? If you have little or no sense of how to run a business, it's time to learn. On-the-job training will teach you the hard way; better to read, research, and study before you become the one-minute manager.

■ Are you self disciplined? It's easy to be excited about getting the cover of *Time* magazine. The great assignments spark an energy that feeds itself. But behind the glitter of those "im-portant" jobs lies your everyday world.

■ As a freelancer you must diligently face the small daily drudgeries with the same aplomb shown those bigger responsibilities. A poor attitude will cripple your work day. Lackadaisical habits will get you into trouble very quickly.

■ There will be mundane tasks and tiresome chores, and your commitment lies here as well. You may be bored by those simple jobs that cover the rent, but you must have the determination to see them through, to make sure they're done right.

■ You should attend to all the "little" tasks with a healthy, positive spirit. There may come a day when you pick and choose only the select commissions, while delegating lesser responsibilities to your assistants. Until then, can you do grunt work and think in the long term?

■ Are you decisive? As the Lord High Everything, you'll be making many decisions and taking responsibility for the consequences. Remember, you are the boss.

■ Does taking a risk scare you? If you can't even chance a response to this question, you've answered it already! Freelancing *is* risky business. After all, it is your time, your energy, and your money being poured into this venture. Professionally, no one else goes down the tubes with you if you fail; personally, you and your family have much to lose.

Outside your studio, it's not a controlled experiment. You may well ask how much luck figures into the equation. I'm one of those who believe that luck is that moment when preparation meets opportunity. You minimize the gamble with sweat and organization, but there are no guarantees and lots of variables. You have to be willing to risk a wager to reap the reward.

■ Can you tolerate a fair amount of rejection? Unfortunately, this is a fact of life for every freelancer up and down the ladder. You will get rejected for many reasons, those misjudgments regarding your abilities probably being the least of your worries.

In simplistic terms, the creative director looks at your work and says, "Can I sell my product with this art? Will I make my point by using this illustration?" If the answer is "no," your work will be rejected.

When all is said and done, it is the portfolio that counts. Remember that rejection is the downside of an isolated opinion, a particular preference. It's not the gospel. I won't kid you. Rejection hurts. But if you have faith in yourself and your ability, rejection will never kill. Create an inner strength from your substantial talent, and draw from it. Rejection is simply part and parcel of freelancing. Can you handle it?

■ Can you thrive on competition? The competition is out there. They're good. They're waiting for you. While this may sound like the promo to a bad slasher flick, it's really not hype or horror. The small army of your skilled peers is tremendously talented, hard working, and organized. In general, I've found the competition to be a rather loose and friendly fraternity. We do play the same game, in the same ballpark. But your comrades-at-arms won't all act like your bosom buddies, nor is that a requirement in their job description.

Competition in free enterprise is the American way. Use it as your motivation and you'll have an edge. Have a keen and healthy esteem for your competition. Respect their work and keep your eyes open: Know what your associates are doing by researching the trade magazines, creative directories, and annuals. Don't be a rubber stamp of the hot new style, but do know what's current. A key to real success is to offer something that's original and fresh—something the buyer can't get just anywhere, from just anybody. Combine this with good service, strengthen it all with determination and forethought, and your competition will not be so scary after all.

■ How do you handle stress? Keep the following buzzwords in mind when pondering the considerable tensions of freelancing: grace under pressure . . . flexibility . . . rolling with the punches . . . shooting from the hip . . . adaptability . . . creativity . . . thinking on your feet. I could go on, but you get the picture.

If you rattle like nuts in a jar when the pressure builds, you're going to be in trouble. The landlord is banging on your studio door; you are certain there'll be a horse's head in your bed the next morning if you don't pay the rent. A once-generous deadline screams at you from

THE TEN COMMANDMENTS OF FREELANCING

1. Thou shalt not say "No." If you don't like the suggestion, work it out amicably. Learn the art of compromise.

2. Thou shalt always communicate in a professional manner. Listen to your client. Educate your client.

3. Thou shalt strive to constantly increase your expertise. Grow and learn; get it better than the day before.

4. Thou shalt relax and have confidence in yourself. Nobody's shooting at you, and you're not doing brain surgery on your mom. Believe in yourself and others will too.

5. Thou shalt make it a point to have fun. Love your profession. Do what you want; work where and when you want, and work with nice people only.

6. Thou shalt have a personal life. Never feel guilty about making (and taking) time for yourself and loved ones.

7. Thou shalt be honest and ethical. Never promise something you can't deliver. And remember: You are selling a product, not your soul.

8. Thou shalt be a good businessperson. Protect your rights by keeping abreast of the ethical standards, laws, and tax reforms. Stay current with pricing guidelines. Learn effective negotiation skills. Maintain excellent records. Don't start a project without paperwork.

9. Thou shalt not take rejection personally. A thick skin and the ability to bounce back are more than clichés in a field where you need those very attributes to *survive*.

10. Thou shalt never miss a deadline! Perhaps the cardinal sin. Be late with a job and chances are you will never be called again by that particular art director.

the calendar while that simple watercolor wash becomes a life or death situation. Panicky?

■ How's your bank book? In times of low pay, slow pay or (heaven forbid) no pay, can you—should you—support yourself and your business with personal savings? Realistically, how long should you do this if your business is new, not up to speed, or in a lull?

My accountant tells me to have a reserve of at least three months in the bank just in case, but everyone's situation is slightly different. Your safety net might be a year or six months. The numbers will vary, but a hard fact remains constant: Can you launch and sustain your business if you're not generating income?

Initially, it may be wiser for you to freelance as a sideline with outside employment (full- or part-time) smoothing the rough financial edges. It's no crime to build towards independence rather then leaping romantically, albeit imprudently, into the fray.

■ Do you mind working alone? Hopefully you have a stunning relationship with the only one sharing your work space—you. Art school is a pleasant memory now—the halls buzzing with kindred spirits spilling into the comfortably familiar studios, a common ground where teachers and students share a singular purpose and excitement. That glorious phase of your life's education is over.

You need to get out and practice those "real world" skills! Life away from the studio, with friends and acquaintances who make actual conversation (and not necessarily shop talk) will help balance the isolation. Outside interests temper the hours you will spend hunched over the drawing table in your own company. Seek activities and nurture a support system outside the studio. You may very well be your own best friend, but don't go it alone.

■ How do you feel about selling yourself? Aside from your artistic responsibilities, this is a salesperson's job. It's a fairly simple situation, at least on paper: You must bring in the work to sustain the business that satisfies your creative impulse.

VALUE OF A STAFF POSITION

Q. *Would a staff position be more helpful at first?*

A. Working on staff will provide invaluable training and experience. It's a perfect atmosphere to hone your skills and perfect your art, and I strongly suggest it. Likewise, you'll need an economic cushion when initiating your freelance venture, so a staff job is a sensible first step.

Benton Mahan, an Ohio illustrator with years of staff and freelance experience, states unequivocally, "I think it's almost impossible to freelance right out of school—or start cold—and make a good income, without doing something else. It's helpful to have the stability, that regular income (of a staff position) when you first start out."

Where better to learn and grow, to discover who you are and where your direction lies? However, development is directly proportionate to the amount of nurturance and challenge you find in your environment. You must interview with your eyes open and a look to the future.

A staff position can be the perfect place to meet and make contacts (but not beg, borrow, or steal clients). But a staff job won't necessarily teach you about the business of freelancing. Unless you interact with freelancers who contract with your company, you may have no idea how these independents actually operate.

If you're a staffer and wish to prepare for freelancing, work yourself into assignments that involve freelancers—and don't balk at added responsibilities; seek them out.

You can gain valuable negotiating skills by sitting at the other side of the table as the art buyer. Relating to clients takes on a new perspective when you are the client yourself.

By getting a job into print, you'll balance brainstorm and budget, guide the bright idea into actual camera-ready art, and deal with the printer to get the desired results on the page. Keeping that aesthetic dream from becoming a lithographer's nightmare garners you technical expertise and practical information about printing costs and pricing.

A staff position can definitely work to your advantage as a freelancer; it's a smart choice. If you're inclined to go this route, you'll be in good company.

MAKING THE BREAK TO FREELANCING

Q. *I am on staff now, but plan to freelance. How do I make the break?*

A. First discuss it with your boss. As long as there are no conflicts of interest with house accounts and your freelancing doesn't interfere with your staff work, there shouldn't be any problem.

But perhaps it's a house rule that staff may not freelance. When you signed your contract, you agreed to abide by company regulations, so honor those terms. Don't believe a discreet, covert operation will remain your little secret for long. The artistic community is smaller than you might think. I guarantee that it'll catch up to you.

It's been said that it's better to look for a new position while you still have your old job. It makes a lot of sense, and only you can decide when (and if) you're ready to make a complete break.

If freelancing is okay with your employer, test the waters first. *Don't* leave on impulse or in anger. Instead, take a few outside assignments and, hopefully, maintain at least one substantial account. Over a period of time, get a taste of the freelance life. When you're mentally prepared, with your financial safety net in place, simply hold your nose and jump!

VALUE OF ART SCHOOL

Q. *Is art school necessary?*

A. Luck may be a small factor where job opportunities are concerned, but not when we're discussing ability. To compete in this field, art education is essential. Learn the basics, pick up the tools, gain the skills necessary to play the game well. Unless your father is Andrew Wyeth, the best place I know to learn all this (in the shortest time period, as painlessly as possible) is art school.

TWO-YEAR VS. FOUR-YEAR PROGRAMS

Q. *Is a two-year commercial art school better than a four-year art program at a university?*

A. The answer depends on your needs and attitudes, your goals and personal timetable. A two-year commercial program is designed to be focused and intense. The four-year university curriculum will be rounded and diverse.

Many university art departments now sponsor a year (usually the junior year) at an affiliated commercial school. This is the best of both worlds for many students. The quality of your art education will not differ in either situation, so the choice of an eclectic university process versus a concentrated commercial approach must be an individual one.

VALUE OF INTERNSHIPS

Q. *Do internships help?*

A. They can. Of course, internships aren't for everyone. Most likely, this will be your first real taste of that particular work experience; but long hours at no pay are not universally appealing. If you're willing to invest your time and energy in some professional training, an internship can be invaluable, just the catalyst to change the course of your life and career. When the opportunity is available and practical to your situation, I wouldn't hesitate to recommend an internship as a smart beginning move.

FEAR OF SELLING

Q. *I dread the thought of selling my work, but I feel I am best suited temperamentally to freelancing. What should I do to overcome this fear?*

A. Illustrator Ben Mahan explains, "You're not alone, but it's just something that you have to do. Most artists can really sell themselves better than anyone else, and you must get out and sell yourself a bit. If you don't like dealing one-to-one, work through the mail. However, you'll need that personal contact, if you can make the connection."

Some artists feel that marketing their work is akin to putting their children up for sale. But first recognize that someone is paying you to produce images for a purpose. And if you remember that you are selling usage of the art rather than the product itself, this anxiety is easily suppressed. Dallas illustrator Mary Grace Eubank cautions you to "realize that you're selling your work, not your soul. Read books on self-projection and confidence building. Possibly attend motivational seminars on sales techniques. Hire a rep and stay in the background until you can develop a more positive persona."

THE FREELANCER'S GAMBLE

Q. *Can you find happiness and security as a freelancer, or do you have to be a hustler all the time?*

A. Your time schedule will hardly be regular, and you're committed to other people's deadlines. There will be moments so quiet you can hear a pen drip, and hectic periods when twenty-four hour days are not enough—hustling is all relative for the freelancer.

Happiness and security? It's my experience that happiness and security in freelancing are achieved by hustling. Perhaps we have given this word a bad connotation. Hustling, as I define it, is nothing more than honest, hard effort. It is aggressively and energetically plying your trade; an assertive attitude combined with a robust work ethic and a good product. My answer is "yes" to both parts of the question.

STAFF SUPPORT

Ernie Norcia is an artist who lives and works in Dayton, Ohio. Assignments for commercial work come to him from a variety of advertising agencies, Gibson Greetings, magazines such as *Sail* and *Small Boat Journal*, and others.

In fact, if you watch television, you've seen Norcia's work. His portrait of Elvis Presley graces the jacket of a record heavily advertised by Time-Life Music. He was also awarded a prime-time "Emmy" as a member of a team of astronomical artists on *Cosmos, The Shores of the Cosmic Ocean*, aired on PBS.

Norcia is an illustrator with a background in education and years of experience as a staff artist. He advises, "In the strictest sense, art school does not provide a 'ticket' into the field. Yet, art school does present an environment for establishing solid work habits, and a prime launch platform for the future. A broad liberal arts education is important for a freelancer. The bigger one's vision, the more that vision can encompass, bettering your chances to handle the incredible variety of requests that will come your way."

After school? "A staff position at an agency or studio would be very helpful in getting a headstart, especially if it's a healthy environment, filled with challenging work and busy, talented people. In such a climate, one receives invaluable instruction in image making.

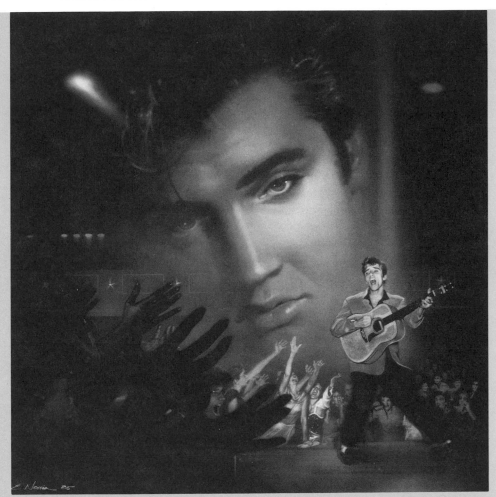

A cold call garnered Dayton artist Ernie Norcia the portfolio review that ultimately led to a first assignment in a mutually satisfying and continuing relationship. Norcia's cover portrait of Elvis Presley for Time-Life Music's *Rock and Roll Era* was one of several to introduce the series and launch an extensive TV and print advertising campaign. Part of a portfolio package he forwards upon request, the evocative Elvis image is included when Norcia needs to demonstrate how he handles a likeness.

"You'll establish good work habits while learning about methods and materials. Feedback on your work is readily available. On staff, one also becomes acquainted with the outside support systems (photographers, stat houses, printing services, typesetters, etc.) and technical shortcuts that help a professional become a professional. Working at a studio or agency will help you identify the potential markets for one's work.

"A staff position is an ideal place to take one's measure before venturing into the national arena. If there are no conflicts of interest with agency accounts, you could freelance on a spot basis while working on staff. But a word of caution: Some companies have strict guidelines for this sort of thing from forbidding it outright to hearty encouragement. Know your company and play by the rules. And remember, if you're leaving a studio to freelance, it's unethical to work with any clients serviced by your former employer for at least six months."

SWITCHING HATS

After eight years as an art director, Elwood H. Smith switched hats to become an illustrator. By this time, Smith had an ulcer from the stress. "Account execs were rushing into the room screaming at you. The job was just wrong for me," he said. "If I didn't break away and do what I wanted to do originally—which was humorous illustration—perhaps, I *couldn't* do it," he realized. "I already lacked a lot of confidence and I thought if I waited any longer, I was a goner."

Today, Smith is arguably one of our premier illustrators. The long road to his signature style began, he says, as a child. "I wanted to be a cartoonist. I used to try to draw Pogo and Walt Disney characters; I used to try to draw like Jack Davis. Our small town in Michigan had no TV 'till I was about sixteen, so I grew up as a radio baby and we traded comics with the other kids. This was early—like the beginning of *Mad*, and the old Barney Google strip in the newspaper. When, down the road, I returned to that as a style, it was very natural, because I really soaked it up as a child."

Smith discovered humorous illustration at the now-defunct Chicago Academy of Fine Arts. He went for two years, without graduating. "I came from a family without much money. I had no backup, I couldn't afford to freelance. Once I got out of school, I had to find a job where I was being paid a salary, and in those days (the early sixties) what you wanted to do was work in a studio—you'd be kind of a gofer, but you'd work your way up."

Smith hit the streets, but couldn't get a job. He says, "It was grueling—I was very shy. Making the phone calls was difficult; going to see people was difficult. Finally, something opened up as an assistant art director in a small publishing house near Chicago."

Two years later, Smith moved back to the city, working as an art director at a Marshall Fields department store for about six months. "I wasn't cut out for that kind of stress, so I worked there for six months, then got a job in an ad agency for about three months. I worked for another ad agency for three years, then decided that I really

A one-man fine arts show called "Happy Hatz" marks Elwood Smith's efforts to stretch beyond what he labels his "transitional Barney Google" style. "I was a little bored," Smith declares, "and dropped out for three months to do my own art, with no limitations. I got very loose, and then applied that to my recent commercial illustration." This piece was printed as a general invitation, but was also sent to all the art directors Smith knew. As a reflection of his later work, Smith tucks a "Happy Hatz" promo in his sample packages. "I am a commercial artist," Smith tells us. "The gallery exhibition was always meant to sell myself as the end product."

wanted to be an illustrator."

Smith shares this history to make an important point: "One thing I can say to the readers is not to be dismayed if you're already in your late twenties and still haven't found a style or don't know in which direction you're going. Moving to Manhattan was the best move I ever made. It wasn't until I came to the city in 1976 at age 35 that I actually had some idea that my style was developing. I didn't have a natural style that just came out. I was all over the place. I had six years of doing illustration in Chicago without really having my own voice."

Smith labels himself a slow learner. "Even the style I brought to Manhattan and used for the first few years," he says, "doesn't really look like what I do now at all. It was very controlled—not that loose approach I now have."

Around this time, illustrator Lou Brooks arrived in New York City. Smith and Brooks shared an affection for comic strips like Krazy Kat and Smoky Stover. "I started buying some of these comics and got very interested in all this old stuff," Smith says. "Lou had a book of Rube Goldberg reproductions. We would look through that and just glow about how great these guys were and how funny. It started seeping into my work. The art directors accepted this loose, cartoony style, and I stayed with it—I think I have it down pretty well now."

Smith has some basic advice for the beginner. "I know every young illustrator can't possibly go to New York City, but I would say if they can, they should. At least for a couple of years. Go to spread your wings, to feel that energy." Having said this, Smith is quick to add, "Remember that success is relative. There are a lot of artists who work in a small market who may never be Mr. or Ms. Famous Illustrator, but they make a nice living. They breathe decent air, have a good life, have a family, and do all the things that are important to people.

"A young person must realize that this is a business. No matter how artsy-shmartsy illustrators are going to be, it's a business. It's called 'commercial art' and it's a real name for something.

"People starting out should do their best work, stand by it, but be quite willing to listen to criticism from art directors. Sometimes, students and young, budding illustrators get too protective about artwork

Smith's "Kartoon Korse" is a promo from *American Showcase*. He routinely uses reprints of this page (and various other directory sheets) in sample packets, mailed upon request to prospective buyers. In addition, every time Smith sends a job to a client, he includes these promotional items as part of the package. "If I work regularly for a person," Smith comments, "they get quite a few; and I hope that they pass the extras on to other people in the art department or agency. 'Kartoon Korse' charmed people more than any promo I've done so far." One of the artist's personal favorites, the ad is a deliberate effort to set his advertising apart from the crowd. The page was not a standard recap of printed assignments, but is a self-contained joke, showcasing Smith's humor and his style. "People use me because of my point of view," he says. "My way of looking at things is slightly askew. The best way to show that was not with jobs drawn for clients, but through work done for myself. I'm trying to get folks to use me for what I do best."

that's not very good. It's a hard balancing act for a beginner—good art directors can share a great deal of wisdom and can probably help you to be better, but a hack designer is not going to get you anywhere."

He has strong feelings about self-promotion. "I've always done it and I've done it well. I had a sense of advertising, a sense of hawking your wares. My philosophy in this business is that you *can't* be too visible.

"Do a self-promotional piece that's memorable and exciting. Make it witty and fun; not too big—8½"x11" or smaller—just something that really sings. Hopefully, the art director will stick it on the wall or, at least, tuck it in their file and you'll be remembered.

"Then, come up with another mailer. Let's say you see an art director in the summer. Around autumn you do this wonderful turkey drawing saying, 'Happy Thanksgiving.' Your name goes 'bing' again. At Christmas you do a Christmas card. Send it out—'bing'—that name hits again. If Bob Jones out there keeps sending those things out, it's going to go 'Bob Jones, bing,' 'Bob Jones, bing,' 'Bob Jones, bing'—and then all of a sudden they're going to call *Bob Jones* instead of Elwood Smith, because they need a little more variety and they say, 'That guy keeps popping up.' "

About the portfolio, Smith says, "If I had listened to everyone when I was first looking for a job in a studio, I would have taken every piece out—so I decided to go by my own instincts.

"Beginning illustrators should avoid putting in life drawings and things they did in school. It makes it look like amateur hour. Don't put in a mixed bag of stuff.

"When I came to New York I had one printed piece. I didn't want to show a mixed bag. I decided that my work should be consistent, and I carried no more than a dozen pieces—they were almost all original pieces, too. When I would do a new piece or get something printed, I would throw one out. It kept my portfolio light.

"A portfolio should be well organized, have a consistent style, and should look good. My portfolio was always very tidy, but I do know illustrators with sloppy portfolios, who stay very busy. There are always exceptions to these rules—but my overall feeling is that most art directors are delighted to get something that looks professional."

What's it like working with art directors? Smith comments, "Some art directors will call you in to do a job. They love your work, but are somehow determined to bend you and the job into the shape that they need. The best art directors don't do that. They wait for the right job and then they call you in for your strength. They don't try to pound your round style into a square format. This happens quite a bit, and I'm constantly resisting that. Sometimes they call me and they're so enthusiastic about using me, that it's infectious; it's hard to say 'no' to someone who's saying, 'Oh, we love you.'

"They're also pretty literal out there. An art director will see something, and they know absolutely that's what they want. So sometimes if they see you do a truck, they'll ask if you can do a bus. This is kind of an old joke among illustrators, but it hasn't changed over the years.

"If you go to the smaller magazines, the ones that use a lot of art but don't pay too much, you often can get a little more freedom as a trade-off, and they'll use you. The smaller publications are good starting points because they'll give young artists a chance. They've got to—they can't get the big names, because they don't have the budgets, so they'll take unknowns and give them a chance.

"When you first start out, you've got to get some work under your belt. No matter how good you are, doing an assignment is quite different from drawing for yourself. The sooner a student can start doing professional work under the demands and confinements of a real situation, the better off they'll be. Work for the small places; get your style pretty well formed, get your chops up, then start hitting the big ones.

"The more work I do, the more it gets out there. The more that gets out there, the more people see. The more people see, the more people use me—it just starts taking care of itself to a certain degree. I don't do mailings for more work because I'm already as busy as I need to be, but I stay real aware that art directors can have short memories."

CHAPTER ONE
CHECKLISTS

Pluses of freelancing:
- ☐ You'll handle a wider variety of more creative assignments.
- ☐ You'll do more of the type of work you want.
- ☐ There's the potential to earn more money.
- ☐ You'll learn to hustle.
- ☐ It's your schedule, even when hours are extended.
- ☐ You decide when to work and for how long.

The minuses of freelancing:
- ☐ Your pay will be erratic.
- ☐ "Professional security" is not applicable.
- ☐ Jobs may not be steady.
- ☐ You'll work alone.
- ☐ The competition is great.

To find out if you have the right stuff for freelancing, ask yourself:
- ☐ What am I getting out of this?
- ☐ Why am I doing this?
- ☐ Do I have a marketable skill?
- ☐ Do I have drive and ambition?
- ☐ How's my business acumen?
- ☐ Am I self-disciplined?
- ☐ Can I do "grunt work" and also visualize the big picture?
- ☐ Am I decisive?
- ☐ Can I take a risk?
- ☐ Can I tolerate rejection?
- ☐ Do I thrive on competition?
- ☐ Can I handle stress?
- ☐ How's my bank book—can/should I support myself and my business with personal savings?
- ☐ Do I mind working alone?
- ☐ How do I feel about selling myself?

How to make the break:
- ☐ Discuss it with your boss.
- ☐ If it's a house rule that staff may not freelance, don't.
- ☐ Look for a 'new position' while you still have your old job.
- ☐ If freelancing is okay with your employer, test the waters.

CHAPTER 2
WHERE DO YOU START?

DEFINITION OF AN ILLUSTRATOR

Q. *What is an illustrator?*

A. Steven Heller and Lita Talarico, in their book *Design Career,* succinctly define illustration as "the painting, drawing, collaging, or sculpting of an image that decorates, complements, or interprets a text or brief." That definition can be broadened by adding that these images can be used in advertising, promotion, industry, manufacturing, media, or specialty publishing.

Illustration is the bridge between the mind's eye and the camera lens; the illustrator builds that bridge when an idea challenges the camera beyond its capacities. An illustrator acts as a conduit of emotion and mood that photography finds elusive. When a concept dictates looking beyond what we perceive as reality, illustration jump-starts the intellectual process to create a world where reality is only regulated by the imagination of the person pushing the media.

DEFINITION OF A GRAPHIC DESIGNER

Q. *What is a graphic designer?*

A. The graphic designer orchestrates type and visuals to communicate, sell, provoke a response, inform, or to educate a mass audience. Bob Bingenheimer, president and owner of his own design studio in Yellow Springs, Ohio, defines it this way, "A graphic designer is a professional trained in communications problem-solving through the use of typography and images. He or she is schooled in printing and communications technologies. Design means organization, and it arose out of the need for an interface between aesthetics and the industrial age. The designer develops communications materials based on knowledge of communication, symbols, and communications technologies."

ILLUSTRATOR VS. DESIGNER

Q. *I'm an illustrator/designer. Should I market myself as both, or just as an illustrator to some companies, a designer to others?*

A. Again, it will be easier — and smarter — to do this on a local level. Granted, it is good for an illustrator to have as much understanding of design as possible, but if you're serious about doing both, you may find it more convenient to market yourself as a designer.

As part of the team, an illustrator will do only one end of a job — the illustrations — but a designer may wear many hats on a project (including snagging the juiciest illustrations). The designer controls the creative flow, while an illustrator may not enjoy the same perks.

Along with the perks will come added responsibilities. Jobs can become so design-intensive the designer may not do any drawing for days or weeks at a time. If you want to be an illustrator, this will present problems, so seriously consider how you're going to sell yourself.

SHOULD YOU DO IT ALL?

Q. *Should you be a jack-of-all-trades or should you concentrate on illustration only?*

A. Many people make good money doing layout and paste-up, plus illustration. Being a jack-of-all-trades would be to your advantage in the beginning, when you may have to do everything to make a living. As your business takes off, you'll eventually concentrate on what you really love to do the best.

ART VS. ILLUSTRATION

Q. *Can you call yourself both an artist and an illustrator?*

A. The late N.C. Wyeth lamented that he was, by his own estimation, "merely" an illustrator. Today we recognize him as a master painter; his oils are considered not only milestones of book illustration but great works of art as well.

I'm not saying you'll be the next Wyeth (his grandson Jamie already has that honor), but I think you can be both artist and illustrator. While there are those who split hairs regarding this terminology, I find the titles interchangeable.

EASING INTO ILLUSTRATION

"Like many other people," Benton Mahan remarks, "I thought I would go into fine art, but illustration just seemed more natural for me."

Mahan, who grew up on a farm in central Ohio, says he was never inside an art museum until he entered college. "My exposure to art was mainly through magazines and books. That's what I can relate to more than paintings."

Mahan majored in illustration, with an advertising minor, and while still in college was offered a job with Hallmark Cards. "They came around to the school recruiting," he tells us. "I didn't take the job at that time. I went to work for a small studio in Columbus, Ohio."

Mahan laments, "It seems there are very few design studios or illustration studios left. When I started out, there were a lot of studios and small design firms that catered to large agencies, but it seems like freelancers have taken over much of that business. There are design firms working in the publishing industry—mainly designing textbooks—and they're giving out a lot of freelance illustration, but there are more freelancers than there ever used to be, and fewer studios."

From Columbus, Mahan moved to New York City and worked for *Industrial Design* as a designer. He eventually talked the powers-that-be into letting him do some spot illustrations for the magazine, his first real illustration assignment.

"While working at the magazine," Mahan says, "I would go out at lunch time and try to pick up other little freelance jobs. I was mainly picking up little black-and-white spots for small magazines. There were some very low-budget small magazines, but, of course, I was hitting everyone I could think of—all the big publishers.

"Most of the art directors were very nice. After I would show them my portfolio, some of them would give me the names of other people to see. Mostly, I used annuals to look up names. I figured these folks win awards, they must be doing a good job—those are the kind of people I want to work with.

"I also worked for a small studio in the city, doing a little bit of everything," Mahan remembers, "but I wasn't getting a lot of big-time freelance jobs."

Returning to Columbus after a year, and remembering the earlier job offer, Mahan relocated to Kansas City, Missouri, where he finally worked for Hallmark Cards.

Benton Mahan's "Postman" dates back to 1979, and was used on a black-and-white mailer sent to Midwestern advertising agencies. The promo was expressly designed to highlight Mahan's black-and-white spot technique. The piece was originally commissioned, but Mahan, wishing to explore the cartoon market, redrew the "Postman" for this particular promotional piece. The black-and-white mailer—often sent in combination with a sleeve of color slides—did the trick, and Mahan received the spot assignments he was after.

Mahan fondly remembers his time in Kansas City. "I learned a lot at Hallmark, and being exposed to the other people who worked there—there are some really great artists at Hallmark. Working in the Contemporary department greatly influenced my humorous illustration.

"I also took part-time classes at the Kansas City Art Institute. I think it's important, when one has time, to keep drawing and painting, picking up new techniques and just learning from other people. I still like taking classes and enjoy discovering what I can. I think drawing is like playing the piano—it takes a lot of practice, and you have to practice continually."

Mahan worked two years at Hallmark before traveling to Europe. "I tried to work in England, which became a bit of a problem, and we wound up going back to New York City."

Mahan started out working for an advertising agency in New York, doing mostly layout. He says, "Eventually, I got to where I was picking up some freelance work, and I started to freelance 'inside' for the advertising agency. This means I would be there at the agency all day, but I was being paid on a freelance basis. They would give me mostly layout and design work and when I didn't have anything to do for them, I could do my illustration work using their facilities.

"I stayed at the agency for awhile. As I started picking up more and more freelance work, I eventually decided to work in my apartment rather than taking the subway every day and enduring the hassle of getting into midtown Manhattan. So I started working out of my studio.

"I went through a couple of reps and finally ran across an agent who seemed to work out well. I didn't have to go out and show my portfolio that much to constantly dig up new assignments, so it allowed me to spend more time working and less time meeting people and showing the book, which is something I really wasn't too thrilled about."

Mahan talks about his early trials and tribulations with candor. "It's always a little difficult when you start out. I kind of phased into it, which I think is the best way to do it. I was living in an area where there was a lot of freelance work available, so I really didn't have too much of a problem keeping busy.

© Benton Mahan. Used with permission.

Mahan had established an ongoing relationship with the art director of *Yankee* when he was called to illustrate an article about a Vermont motorcycle convention. He now includes the piece in his portfolio and also on a promotional flyer. "People find it quite humorous, and I feel it makes a strong statement. The piece always gets a big reaction."

"My wife was working at the time. That gave us a steady paycheck and also gave us insurance. One of the biggest problems of freelancing is you have no disability insurance, no life insurance, or health insurance. You have to pay all your own Social Security; you have to pay your income tax quarterly; and sometimes you have to wait a long time to be paid on a job. That's what makes starting out in illustration a little tougher, but it wasn't too bad for me. Because I had a steady income working in the advertising agency and gradually kind of phased into freelance, it wasn't a *big* problem."

How does Mahan maintain his freelance business? "The most extensive self-promotion I do," he tells us, "is to put an ad in *American Showcase* every year. That gives me two thousand reprints.

"I have a small mailing list. I've bought mailing lists in the past and sent out mailers, but it seems I get very little response from sending out a lot of mailers. I get more response from people looking through the *Showcase* or from clients I've developed.

"I'll pinpoint someone I'd like to work for and call them up; I'll send slides or mailers (the reprints are mainly what I use now) and pursue a client until I find out it's going to be a dead end or they send me some work.

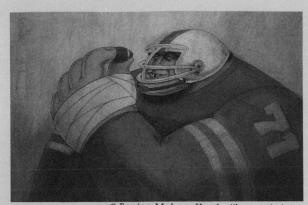

© Benton Mahan. Used with permission.

Mahan's "Football Player" has been sold a number of times to different magazines. Initially a personal sample, the piece drew a great response, prompting Mahan to use it as self-promotion. When the drawing sold initially, Mahan was careful to retain all reproduction rights, enabling him to sell the image to other interested art buyers. As he is selling second reproduction rights, Mahan offers the drawing at a reduced rate (usually fifty percent of the original fee).

"I get a lot of repeat business. The way my self-promotion differs now than when I started is that I have full-color mailers to send out. In the beginning, I only had black and white and slides. I still send out slides because sometimes people want to see more specific things. A greeting card company wouldn't be as interested in my *Showcase* mailer because it's more editorial illustration.

"I don't have a full-color mailer geared to greeting cards. I have a tendency to send slides or card samples to the card companies. Card companies also seem to be able to relate to children's books I've done, so those make good samples to send as well."

As an active freelancer and part-time illustration instructor at his alma mater, the Columbus College of Art and Design, what is Ben Mahan's advice to beginning freelancers? "You must think of this as a business," he says, "and that your artwork is the product you are producing. Deadlines are very important. Someone can live with a piece of art that is not quite perfect, but they can't live with a blank page in a magazine. You have to think about the client's needs. You have to be someone who is easy to work with. Nobody wants to work with a prima donna or someone who's difficult.

"There are a lot of artists out there. You have to bid on jobs, and it's always good to keep in touch with people. Something may come up and they might not think to call you.

"Follow up on all jobs—see if they like it. Make an art director feel that he or she is the only client you work for, that you're doing your best effort for them. When you send a job in, it should always be neat, clean, and well presented. If you mail the artwork, remember that you're responsible for getting it there. Package the piece well and insure it.

"Always answer the problem that the art director set out for you to answer. When someone calls, find out what the job pays. Many places have you bid on the job. Some places have a set fee. If you bid, get all the information possible, and get a layout so you know what you're bidding on. Find out how your imagery is to be used—are they going to make one ad out of it, is it going to be used on billboards, T-shirts, everything you can think of. Price depends on usage—is it a national or a local client? If you're doing an ad for Bob's Service Station, it's not going to pay as much as if you're doing an ad for Exxon."

Mahan leaves us with a final thought. "One more thing I should mention, this is the perfect job for me. If I were smarter I might do something that required some kind of intelligence, or if I were stronger I might do some kind of manual labor. This is the perfect job. I can sleep in the morning, work at home, and just go out to the mailbox and get checks."

Humorous illustrator Sam Viviano dislikes the label "fine" art. Viviano says, "It's as if the commercial arts are not particularly fine—in the sense of meaning good—and that the fine arts are not particularly commercial. Unfortunately, the public in general, and too many artists, buy into this." Instead, Viviano uses the germs "graphic" and "gallery" arts. "What's really different is whether one's art hangs on a wall or is intended for reproduction."

FINDING THE RIGHT MARKETS

Q. *How do I analyze what market is right for me?*

A. First, consider what you like to do the best. Then take a walk to the local library, followed by a trip to the newsstand. See who's doing what and how they're doing it. Research who's publishing what and what is being published. Evaluate your work in light of the marketplace's current needs and trends, and take some notes.

Freelancers with strong political convictions and the passionate need to express those views will find their work fits current affairs magazines and newspaper op-ed sections.

If you have the eye of a storyteller, look to magazine and book illustration to challenge that sharp sense of visual narrative.

Perhaps pictorial commentary is not your thing. A light, whimsical drawing style will keep you in great demand at greeting card companies. You'll also sell to book publishers, magazines, newspapers, advertising agencies, and design studios.

Every market has an enormous need for a wide variety of styles and sensibilities. Look to your head and heart to tell you where your direction lies, then explore what markets fit your criteria.

STARTING LOCALLY

Q. *I am an illustrator. Should I start locally or try national markets? What are the best markets for a beginner to try?*

A. Start locally and small, but with an eye on the national markets and the big time. Learn to conduct business at home, then use this training to branch out beyond your own turf.

You shouldn't limit yourself to local clients. After all, it's just as easy to mail a package across the country as it is around town. But there are good markets waiting for you, and literally right down the street.

Local businesses, with needs ranging from advertising or promotional material to signage and stationery, are excellent markets for the beginner. Case in point:

- The public television station may need you to energize the mailers for their current fund drive.
- Local magazines are always on the lookout for images.
- Professors at the university could use an artist to pump life into those classroom handouts for next semester.
- Your neighborhood newsletter would jump at the chance for some snappy drawings.
- Advertising agencies all over town need art on a continual basis. Call them!
- The corner deli is looking for a new graphic identity.
- A dentist, interested in stationery and letterheads, also needs a catchy cartoon on the front of her check-up reminders.
- An insurance company wants to soften payment notices and complement other mailed material with humorous illustration. Their in-house magazine regularly uses visuals, too.

It's easy to see that good assignments are there to be found. Keeping that in mind, I'd look to your own backyard for those first jobs. (For more on working with local businesses, see Chapter 11.) With this invaluable experience, moving to the national markets will be that much easier.

MOVING TO ANOTHER SMALL TOWN

Q. *I'm new in town. I'd been freelancing in the small town we left, then I moved with my husband to another small town. How do I get started again? Would this be a good time to expand my horizons regionally?*

A. Publicity is the name of the game right now. Advertise in the local newspaper; you might even consider an announcement on your cable

DOING IT AS A DUO

In the mid-fifties, as illustration became more conceptual, Simms Taback found himself influenced by a group of New York graphic designers who called themselves Push Pin Studios. "I looked towards Push Pin for what was creative, what was new, what was energetic in illustration," Taback says.

At Push Pin were names like Edward Sorel, Milton Glaser, and Seymour Chwast. Another of its founding members was Reynold Ruffins.

Ruffins and Taback graduated from Cooper Union. Both spent years working on staff (at a variety of agencies and studios) before making the break to full-time freelance illustration in the sixties. They still work together in their New York City studio, sharing a tradition of good graphic design plus a wealth of knowledge and experience.

MCF: Where does a beginner get started?
Taback: "On staff. It's good, solid experience and a benefit for somebody who is thinking of being a freelancer.

"I think there's only one market in which to begin. That's to do editorial work for the hundreds of different specialty magazines that are around. That's the market. You don't have much choice when you're new. The fees are small, they're looking for beginners, they're on the cutting edge of new stuff—they're interested in what the art schools are turning out. That is the market for the beginners, not the agencies."
Ruffins: "Just out of school, those people who live in small towns probably have a very good chance with the smaller agen-

cies. It's probably more one-on-one. In many cases, they can go directly to different companies in the area and offer their services."

MCF: As illustrators who have been both art directors and graphic designers at one point or another, define the titles "Art Director" and "Graphic Designer."
Ruffins: "An art director might be more conceptual. He or she would think of an idea, pick a typeface, choose an illustrator, pull the different elements together. An illustator never does any design."
Taback: There's an old Herb Lubalin story. An art director brings his work home to show his mother. He says, 'Look, Ma, look what I did.' The mother says, 'Herbie, what did you do? Did you make the picture?' He says, 'No, Ma, I didn't make the picture.' She says, 'Did you make the type?' He says, 'No, Ma, I didn't make the type.' She says, 'Did you do the writing?' He says, 'No, Ma, I didn't do the writing.' She says, 'Well, what did you do, Herbie?' *That's* what an art director is!"
Ruffins: "A graphic designer does less advertising work and more work in publications. Art directors work in ad agencies, and graphic designers often have their own studios. Many freelance. The graphic designer probably has a better knowledge of design, and talent at pulling design elements together."

MCF: Can a beginner market himself as both a designer and an illustrator?
Taback: "I don't think you can do both successfully. If you want to be both an illustrator and a designer, be a designer. Sell yourself as a designer and you'll create a market for your illustration. Milton Glaser, like Seymour Chwast a brilliant illustrator, has always said he's a graphic designer, *because that's how the world needs to understand you.*

"Reynold and I have done the other thing. We've minimized the graphic design, and sold ourselves as illustrators. You have to present some clarity to people; it just confuses them—you have to be one thing or the other."

MCF: You once worked together as a graphic design studio. Why label yourself as illustrators rather than designers?
Taback: "The illustration business is a sim-

pler business in a sense. It's you doing everything yourself. A graphic design business can be rather large, if it's really successful.

"The purpose of forming a graphic design business is *not* to be a one-person shop. You want to actually have a *business,* get various kinds of work and do a whole lot of different projects at the same time. It's a different operation, really. If you're going to be a communications company, then it's moving in an entirely different direction.

"The only people who work as graphic designers *and* illustrators are book jacket designers. They have a small, one- or two-person operation and are, in a sense, generalists. They're a graphic designer/illustrator, and this is how they function in the business."

MCF: How does a beginner find the right market for his or her work?
Taback: "This is a business of people. Look at the annuals and directories—you'll see the kind of work that's being used, who's using it, and where your work might fit in. Any market can use any type of work. It really depends on the thinking of the people who conceive the ideas."
Ruffins: "I think there's a world of difference in markets, for example, advertising and editorial. In advertising, most of the stuff is pre-solved. I'm being a little crude about this, but you're used as a pair of hands. In an ad agency the idea is usually shown to the client before they go ahead to the finish. The idea is already worked out, sketched up, shown, and approved—*then* they call in the illustrator to use his style to solve the problem."
Taback: "There are some illustrators who are idea-oriented, editorial-type illustrators who wouldn't do well in advertising. Reynold and I do advertising and editorial, and bend to both needs."

MCF: Do freelancers who live in a big city have a better chance at success than those who live in small towns?
Taback: "There is an advantage to being closer to the market. I'd say that people who live in the big city probably have an edge."
Ruffins: "There are many freelancers who live outside the city, but I think you have to be in touch with one of the big cities. You

"Editorial Importance" was one component of a very effective campaign New York illustrator Simms Taback drew for *Electronics* magazine. "Editorial Importance" became part of a mini-portfolio—one of a successful series of three. The small black-and-white booklets displayed a variety of images and showcased a range of line styles. Produced in conjunction with Taback's rep, the mini-portfolios (sent self-contained in individual envelopes) were targeted to advertising agencies from a list generated by Taback's agent.

have to get work from the larger market areas—no matter where you're living—if you're going to be successful. It's probably pretty hard, though manageable, to live in a small place and get all your income from that particular area; I think eventually you'd want to get it from other market areas."

MCF: What advice would you give to beginning illustrators?
Ruffins: "Young people coming out of school usually show *everything*—photographs, nudes—and that's just *not* what an

© Reynold Ruffins. Used with permission.

Reynold Ruffins' "Johnny Appleseed" was done for a calendar earmarked to become a children's book. The New York-based illustrator was working with writer Jane Sarnoff at this time. The partners were asked by Scribners to do a kids' how-to book on bicycle repair, which really opened the door for them to do their own thing.

"After this assignment," Ruffins says, "the publisher was responsive to ideas that we generated ourselves." The series of projects that followed gave Ruffins the opportunity to play with a style he was later able to use in advertising. "The vehicle of children's books," Ruffins comments, "granted me the freedom to work the way I wanted."

Done as separate plates, "Johnny Appleseed" broke down very conveniently into black-and-white and color elements. It was used as a successful promo.

art director wants to see. The students are so eager to show that they're talented, they show too much.

"Show a portfolio with some consistency—don't show life drawings *and* book jackets. Make it the very best you have, but be highly discriminating. Leave out things that aren't absolutely germane to the place to which you're going."

Taback: "The most important thing is the portfolio. You have to have outstanding work—*interesting* work with a point of view. Some call this a style. Your book must have character and be different than the next guy's. Hone the portfolio down so it has a strong look, otherwise, no one will remember it."

Ruffins: "You can't overemphasize a sharp, clean, neat presentation. It's so important. There are people with good heads, but sloppy books. Others may not be as talented, but have a neat presentation—this person is probably more valuable to an art director, because he leaves a better impression with the general audience."

MCF: Can you find happiness and security as a freelancer or do you have to be a hustler all the time?

Ruffins: "Oh, dear . . . we're kind of laid back. We're just not as aggressive—I'm not as aggressive."

Taback: "We ain't hustlers! But I think we had a good time—right, Reynold? We don't feel that *secure* all the time. I'll tell you something—it's a tremendous privilege to do what you like to do. Most of the time, we like what we're doing, so it makes us fairly happy. The security part, that *is* the problem with freelancing. It's being unemployed most of the time! You're only as good as your last job—at least that's the feeling you have.

"You always wonder while you're working on something—you're counting how many jobs you have waiting for you, and when you're down to your 'last one.' I was speaking to the wife of one of the most successful illustrators in this business, and I inquired, 'How's your husband? Give him my regards.' She tells me, 'Oh, he's a little worried lately because he's working on his last job.' I asked, 'What do you mean, his last job?' And she says, 'We don't have anything on the board.'

"The moral here is that we *all* feel insecure—using that time constructively will be the answer. Instead of sitting around worrying, use the time to promote yourself. That's the trick."

Ruffins: "You can be successful at this business if you satisfy a client's needs. But if you keep, above all, the desire and the obligation to satisfy your *own* needs and use the client as a vehicle, then I think you're going to be a lot happier in this business. You must balance doing what you want to do while making it a saleable product."

Taback: "What Reynold's saying is that it's a two-way track. When you take on an assignment you have to ask yourself two questions: 'Can I fulfill the assignment?' and 'How can I use it to . . .'"

Ruffins: ". . . fulfill myself?"

Taback: "Right. Will it be interesting to *me?* Just be clear about it. Sometimes, to be very blunt, you do a job because you can do it quickly and it pays a good fee, then you go on to the next one. That is a reason to do a job, or it's not a reason to do a job — but at least be clear that that's what's happening there.

"Or you're not getting paid enough for a job but it's interesting. I might have a nice sample and I might really enjoy it. *That's* a reason to do a good job. Either accept it or reject it, but be clear that that's why you're doing it. If you're always clear in terms of what you're getting out of it, I think you'll just fare better over the hills and valleys."

channel's community calendar or a late, late night television spot (when ad rates are dirt cheap). Organize that mailing program. Tell your new neighbors to spread the word around. Join the local art organizations and schmooze. Stuff mailboxes or stick flyers on windshields. Check at the chamber of commerce, where they can refer you to potential clients who need your work. Let your fingers do the walking and make cold calls. The idea is to tell the business community who you are, what you do, and where to find your services.

At this point, it's a relatively short hop to go regional, but I wouldn't until you've established a home base—professionally and personally. The markets aren't going away, they'll be there when you're comfortably situated and in position to solicit their business.

BIG CITY, BRIGHT LIGHTS?

Q. *Do freelancers who live in a big city have a better chance at success than those who live in small towns?*

A. Regardless of location, your shot at success will not be the proverbial "piece of cake," and not many years ago, the answer would've been a resounding "yes!"

Today, the answer is still yes. But the proliferation of phone answering services, phone answering machines, express mail couriers, computers, word processors, modems, and burgeoning fax machines supplies an out-of-town freelancer with tools to effectively set up shop in any city, just about anywhere.

Success can be elusive wherever you operate. Living in New York City, considered the hub of the industry, doesn't guarantee a cushy career. It's a bit like peeling the layers of an onion, and defining what qualifies you as a success is relative and rather subjective. The busy freelancer getting $30 to $40 an hour may be tickled to earn this money, until he talks to an illustrator making over $60,000 a year. That fellow discovers a colleague who casually drops the bomb that she earned even more while working half the assignments (and with a month's vacation to boot)! This woman is awed by the big-name illustrator she encountered who netted at least $300,000 last year.

FIFTEEN QUICK AND EASY WAYS TO LOSE CLIENTS

1. "Drop by" without an appointment or "pop in" unexpectedly.

2. Don't return phone calls or answer your mail. Don't follow up. Delay sending requested samples. In the same spirit, arrive late for meetings.

3. Push your wares too fast or so hard that you are insensitive to the client's needs and wants (while remaining overly sensitive to your own).

4. Be overconfident, arrogant, or rude. Always project a negative attitude and unpleasant demeanor.

5. Act intimidated or lack confidence.

6. Give a slipshod, unprofessional presentation. If you still get the job after this, do sloppy work.

7. Copy someone else's art or present work that is not your own.

8. Don't listen to the client. Don't ask questions. Then don't follow directions.

9. Overprice. Then turn in a bill that's larger than the quote.

10. Whine, whimper, or balk at suggestions.

11. Require the client to do more work than is their responsibility.

12. Fluster easily, consistently panic.

13. Promise more than you can deliver; give less than what was asked.

14. Miss a deadline.

15. Do bad work.

She vows that she, too, will be just as successful.

You get the picture. Your chances for success may be better if you live in the big city. Without a doubt, there is more work in one New York City block than in all of Yellow Springs, Ohio. But the relaxed quality of life in this friendly, tranquil spot cannot be found anywhere in New York. It's a trade-off artists living and working here have made without a second thought.

It's definitely easier to market your services on the spot, as opposed to marketing from a remote location. Realistically, small-town freelancers wanting to market illustration in the big city will meet challenges of time and distance their metropolitan brothers and sisters don't face. But it can be done.

How? With talent, of course, but talent alone is no guarantee of success. Rather, the key is your ability, plus lots of elbow grease, coupled with intensive customer service and energetic marketing and self-promotion.

WORKING WITH NEW BUSINESSES

Q. *Should I work with new or established businesses?*

A. Both, but some words of caution here: Be careful when taking an assignment with a new business (new ones frequently fail and don't pay), and do your homework prior to working for any company, regardless of track record. Chances are very good that that pioneering enterprise or established organization will treat you right, but reputation—or bright promise, for that matter—is no guarantee that this firm will be a dream client.

The best offense is always a strong defense. Take good notes over the phone. If you're a terrible note taker, buy an answering machine with two-way record. Ask incisive questions at the meeting. Be prepared to discuss your rates and evaluate how the client's needs jibe with yours. It's best to clarify terms right at the start.

About bids and estimates—don't be pressured into talking money or cutting the deal on the spot; when you need the time, take it. Excuse yourself for ten minutes, say, "I'll call you back in an hour," tell the client you'll have the figure for them on Wednesday or whatever. Just take the time to work out a realistic bid. Don't be afraid to ask for what you really need to do the assignment; be prepared to say no and maybe lose the job. Approach all negotiations with open eyes and mind. Remember that negotiation is a bit of a game and it's all a learning process. Nobody's shooting at you. Actually, life is one long negotiation, so you're fairly seasoned already.

Drawing up a purchase order, or written documentation of some sort, at the beginning of a job is wise. If you don't get a contract on the outset of an assignment (or the client is simply slow with the paperwork), do it from your end. Send a letter of confirmation yourself. This can simply be a short thank-you note outlining the terms of the agreement and job specifications—no legalese, just plain, polite talk spelling out the arrangement made between the illustrator and art buyer.

Let's say the client looks shaky for some reason and you still take the job (brave soul). You can minimize your risk by asking for payments at various points of completion. This could be half on signing and half on delivery or the finished work, or one-third at the beginning, one-third on acceptance or roughs, and one-third upon delivery of the final.

But why bother in the above scenarios? If your experience, radar, or research tells you a buyer is dubious, you don't really need the aggravation or the bucks. There is no adequate compensation for time spent in hell, despite the invaluable lesson learned. Better to politely decline and move on. If the potential pay-off proves too alluring, know what you're getting into and strap on your seatbelt—it's going to be a long, interesting ride before you see that money.

HOW TO NETWORK

Q. *What is networking? How do you do it? Does it pay off? What can I learn from other freelancers? How do I find other freelancers in my town?*

A. The one thing everybody has, and almost always loves to give away, is advice. Yes, it's okay to seek advice; don't shy away or sniff at this informal information gathering.

Networking is a low-key, direct means of communication that pays handsome dividends because there is much to learn from other freelancers.

Your fellows are veritable storehouses of information. Frankly, it can be downright fun to compare notes with someone sharing the same experience. Most contacts enjoy talking shop and are easy to find. Locally, start with the Yellow Pages under "Artists" (commercial and fine arts) or "Graphic Designers." If you go national, research the creative annuals (like *American Illustration* or *The Society of Illustrators)* and talent directories such as *American Illustration Showcase, Creative Black Book, RSVP,* and *The Graphic Artists Guild Directory.* These volumes are invaluable references highlighting the best of the best. They're a wonderful source of inspiration and will supply addresses and phone numbers.

How to network? Regardless of method (by letter or phone) or scope, the formula is simple: Introduce yourself, make friendly conversation while asking pertinent questions, acquire other names and numbers, and then repeat the process. Keep in touch with everybody.

The results? Stimulating ideas and information, new colleagues, and fresh contacts. Illustrator Mary Grace Eubank reminds us, "I'm a firm believer in what goes around, comes around. Keep track of whom you contact and be aware of how they can help you. Don't feel guilty about using these connections. Most artists are receptive and helpful. You must do the same."

Why network only with other illustrators? If a knowledgeable source is willing and available, talk to an editor, art or design director, or a production coordinator (even when you're not involved on a job). Don't forget typesetters or layout artists. How about the pressman at the printers? Approach the sales manager, too. If you really want some insider information, talk to any secretary, assistant, or clerk!

Don't ask other artists to analyze or dissect their methodology for you. Don't call to promote a free drawing lesson. I have sometimes discussed materials (common window shopping) when networking, but I draw the line at process.

While most of your conferees will be happy to chat, or will politely decline, you'll inevitably run into those who virtually accuse you of stealing state secrets. Remember that tough competition and the drive to succeed may create surprising attitudes. Credit that person for their interesting perspective, thank them for their fascinating advice, and say good-bye.

VOLUNTEERING

Q. *I've been told that volunteering my art services to good causes will help. Does it?*

A. Most definitely. You will:

- Gain confidence at the drawing board doing actual assignments.
- Have creative freedom without any pressures to cut the best deal.
- Design according to your vision.
- Learn about deadlines and working with a client.
- Acquire a printed piece for your portfolio, work experience for your resume, and achieve name recognition.
- Get profitable leads, make new contacts, and establish a reputation as someone willing to go the extra mile.
- Have the happy and satisfying experience of completing a job done well for a worthwhile purpose.

You'll find established artists donating their services, so don't look at volunteering as merely paying your dues. Far from it. It's a healthy investment of time, energy, and spirit for any artist, regardless of professional stature.

REFERRALS

Q. *How do I get referrals?*

A. If you do your best work, meet your deadlines, and are dependable, the referrals will take care of themselves.

Referrals come in two varieties: as leads and as references. To get a reference, you'll need a few jobs under your belt first. These referrals usually are the result of a rewarding and positive performance. The client likes your illustration and passes the word on: "This is the person to see to get the assignment done right. Call her!"

Leads often accompany references. The satisfied client above not only refers you to one compatriot, but supplies you the name and address of yet another businessperson needing your services. A graphic designer gives you a hot tip that the design studio across town is looking for an artist of your caliber right away. You make the phone call, mention your contact, and arrange a portfolio review. You call the art director on your last job and network a little—"Do you know anybody who knows anybody who needs anybody?" This art director, more than happy to help, gives you a list of five new contacts. It's now up to you.

WORKING IN THE BIG CITY

With dreams of being a rich and famous illustrator, Sam Viviano moved to New York from Michigan at the end of 1975. Fresh out of college, he had a portfolio made up of everything he had ever done, from block letter forms and theater posters to photographs of abstract expressionist canvases.

"It took me a while to understand the market here. While it may not be true everywhere, to really survive in New York—and in the national market—you have to specialize. After a month of seeing art directors, I realized that I just didn't have the appropriate portfolio for an illustration career. I wasn't going to be rich and famous in a month. I had to do something in the meantime."

The meantime was working as a textile designer for a year. During that year, Viviano asked himself these questions: What do you do best? What do you enjoy doing most? What do you think you can sell? His answer was the same for all three questions: caricature. He developed a new portfolio skewed towards caricature. Freelance illustration became his goal, but he stayed with his full-time job.

"I got my first freelance assignment by answering an agency ad in the *New York Times*. The job turned out to be for a softcore porno comedy, a bad parody of Elvis Presley. In spite of what it was, it was my first job—and it was a movie poster! My idea was to do a terrific job (no matter how bad the project). It would still be a wonderful portfolio piece. I took it very seriously."

The ad agency sent Viviano directly to the producer of the film. "Working in advertising can be a pain, but usually the pain is relatively short, because they're dealing with a deadline. This thing went on for about two and a half months. It dragged on and on through three sets of full sketches. Each time the producer said the caricature didn't look enough like Elvis—although the lead looked nothing like Presley. Finally, I just drew Elvis and, of course, the producer said, 'It looks too much like Elvis!'"

A sketch was eventually approved. "Once again, I worked as hard as I possibly could on the finish. I was very happy with it, but the producer still made changes. I had to do overlays and patches until it was something I absolutely hated. For two and a half months of work I got $235. But, of course, a job is a job."

Viviano feels that the beginner can't avoid going down blind alleys, but says, "If you're smart, you learn from everything you do, not only aesthetically, but also in a business sense."

He strongly cautions beginning artists not to put anything into their portfolio that they don't want to do. "Ask yourself twice: Is it worth doing something I don't like in order to make a lot of money? If this is your priority, go to law school. The likelihood of making a lot of money as an artist is pretty slim. I would guess that the average illustrator probably makes well under $30,000 a year—I'm talking full-time illustrators—maybe even significantly less than that. The number that we informally bandy about at the Graphic Artist's Guild is $20,000.

"If you're going to work in a specialist's market (like New York), and you go out with a generalist's portfolio, each one of your pieces competes with hundreds of people who specialize in just what that piece is all about. You multiply your competition with each shift in approach and style.

"Address the needs of your marketplace. Accept the fact that you won't get the big money or high-profile work (*Time, Esquire, Reader's Digest*, etc.) right away. Get exposure, but more importantly, explore your media and the way you see the world. Style has everything to do with this vision—the way you analyze what you see, and the way you put that down on paper. For the beginning professional, every single job should be an enormous learning experience. Make this personal growth a career-long goal.

Viviano's promo spread in *American Showcase* was originally commissioned by Scholastic's *Dynamite* magazine for a readers' poll of favorite movie actors, television stars, and cartoon characters. When asked to do five or six subjects, Viviano—with a mind toward that future promotional piece—drew practically the whole list. "I worked hard to do a good job and, indeed, this is a strong piece," Sam remarks. "It represents me well, and basically says what I do—caricature."

© Sam Viviano. Used with permission.

"It doesn't matter how talented you are if nobody knows about it. I do think that a certain prejudice exists that if you've got a New York address, somehow you're a better illustrator than somebody who lives in Akron, Ohio. I think it's much truer now that you can have a very big, national reputation without having gotten near New York. My favorite example is Jared Lee, who lives in Lebanon, Ohio. You can't get smaller town than that, but he's learned how to market himself on a national level.

"Self-promotion is an absolute necessity, but the form it takes varies. I think beginners haven't yet hammered out what they want to say about the world they see and how they want to say it. For the newcomer to pay thousands of dollars to be in some trade directory is really putting the cart before the horse.

"Take whatever it costs and get some cards made. You could even go to the photocopy place and run off hundreds of nice black-and-white fliers. Then address the market for which you think you're most appropriate.

"Understand that one visit or one reminder may not be enough, and realize that art directors actually have real jobs. They're working full-time. Looking at people's portfolios is only part of their job.

CHAPTER TWO
CHECKLISTS

How to analyze the right market for your skills:
- ☐ Consider what you like to do best.
- ☐ Go to the local library, followed by a trip to the newsstand.
- ☐ Look at everything.
- ☐ Study printed material.
- ☐ Evaluate your work in light of the marketplace.
- ☐ Look to your head and heart to tell you where your direction lies, then explore those markets that fit your criteria.

Contact these local businesses:
- ☐ The public television station.
- ☐ Local magazines on the lookout for images.
- ☐ Professors at the university.
- ☐ Your neighborhood newsletter.
- ☐ Advertising agencies.
- ☐ The corner deli.
- ☐ The dentist.
- ☐ An insurance company (and their in-house magazine).

To expand your horizons regionally:
- ☐ Advertise in the local newspaper.
- ☐ Put an announcement on your cable channel's community calendar.
- ☐ Consider a late night television spot.
- ☐ Organize that mailing program.
- ☐ Tell your new neighbors to spread the word.
- ☐ Join local art organizations.
- ☐ Stuff mailboxes or stick flyers on windshields.
- ☐ Check at the chamber of commerce for new businesses.
- ☐ Make cold calls.

On working with new or established businesses:
- ☐ Be careful when taking an assignment with a new business, since new ones frequently fail and don't pay.
- ☐ Do your homework prior to working for any company, regardless of track record.
- ☐ Use sound business practices: Take good notes over the phone and ask incisive questions at the meeting; Evaluate how the client's needs jibe with yours. Be up front and crystal clear about terms right at the start.

How to network:
- ☐ Start with the Yellow Pages under "Artists" (commercial and fine arts) or "Graphic Designers."
- ☐ Research the creative annuals and talent directories.
- ☐ Introduce yourself; make friendly conversation while asking pertinent questions; acquire other names and numbers; then repeat the process. Keep in touch with everybody.
- ☐ Talk to an editor, art or design director, production coordinator, typesetter or layout artist, the pressman, sales manager, secretary, assistant, or clerk.
- ☐ Don't ask other artists to analyze or dissect their methodology.

CHAPTER 3
HOW DO YOU GET NOTICED?

SELF-PROMOTION

Q. *Is self-promotion necessary?*

A. Self-promotion is essential, not just to get work, but to get the work you want. Pure and simple, self-promotion is blowing your own horn—letting people know who you are, what you do, and reminding them.

I'm a firm advocate of marketing and self-promotion. It will require much organization and discipline, plus a financial investment—and it's worth every ounce of energy, every minute, and every penny you will spend.

Sounds serious, huh? Yes, it is, but also lots of fun! Self-promotion is a fact of life for the freelancer. With so many good illustrators out there, it's absolutely crucial.

New York illustrator (and ex-art director) Peter Spacek has this advice, "Do a large scale mailing immediately! A full-on attack will spread your name around and will make you an 'entity'—it suddenly gives you illustrator status, even if you've never done a paid job in your life."

SELF-PROMOTION ON A LIMITED BUDGET

Q. *What self-promotional materials should you concentrate on with a limited budget?*

A. No one can afford to send transparencies to all the names on a large mailing list. The answer obviously lies in print.

Smaller budgets dictate smart decisions. You want your promotional package to be economical, but not to look cheap. Good graphics do not have to mean expensive four-color extravaganzas. In the hands of a first-rate printer, well designed and executed line art will look great.

With present technology, a promo reproduced on a high-quality photocopier can be even easier on your wallet. Explore the new color photocopiers, too; the results are good, and the costs are reasonable.

ASSEMBLING YOUR SELF-PROMOTIONAL PACKAGE

Q. *How do you put your self-promotional package together?*

A. Any self-promotion requires a battle plan, but limited resources mandate that you do your homework before getting your promotion off the ground. Study your mailing list and develop a strategy: Determine what you'll be sending (cards, a brochure, flyers—in what combination?), the sequence of events, and when to act. Tally the number of pieces you need (including leftovers for future handouts).

Next, determine the variety and frequency of your anticipated mailing program. To do this, you need to investigate expenses. With your numbers and needs in mind, find a good typesetter and printer (or locate that quick print center with the fine photocopier). Obviously, if you're a colorist, you should be advertising in color at some point. To reproduce color correctly, you'll need a first-rate color separator (if your budget is especially tight, opt for a color photocopier).

How does one locate these folks? The first step is to consult the phone book. Also, get recommendations and referrals from anyone who buys print on a regular basis—fellow artists, graphic designers, any business that advertises. Make appointments to look at samples in general and to discuss your job in particular. Find the best work at the best price and get the show on the road.

Sit down with your contact and assess exactly what your ideas will cost and what work you can do to defray the end figure. Now, start tailoring that scheme to fit your budget. When faced with cold facts and figures, your whole concept may do a 180-degree turn. Roll with it, and don't be surprised when you come up with a different (and better) plan! Yes, you may have to streamline, but limited finances should only force you to maximize your strategy. Getting the most value for your dollar does not necessarily mean shopping in the bargain basement.

PRESENTING A VISUAL IDENTITY

Q. *How do you present a professional image?*

MASTERING SELF-PROMOTION

To many of his peers, illustrator Jared Lee of Lebanon, Ohio, is considered a master of self-promotion. Lee says, "I'm a firm believer in advertising yourself. As artists, we're in the advertising business. I would hope we believe in it as much as anybody. Over half my work is for advertising agencies, so most of the drawing I do is promoting a product. If my clients quit believing in advertising, I've got a real problem."

Lee started his business in 1970. He worked with Gibson Greeting Cards for about a year, then struck out on his own. It took time to build his business through self-promotion and contacts in the industry.

Lee clearly remembers the trials and tribulations he faced as a beginner. "Everything's much easier now. When I started out, there were no books like the *Creative Black Book* or *American Showcase*. You didn't have any mailing lists you could buy, so you had to compile your own."

So how *does* the master of self-promotion promote himself? "I don't send out promotion pieces and wait by the phone. I never send out a promotion piece to get a particular job." He sends out pieces to attract a particular type of client through a targeted campaign.

"As a beginner, I didn't have the budget to use four color, but now my promotional pieces are full color. But even if your promo is black and white, you want it to look sharp. Yours is not the only piece an art director gets that day. It's very competitive; there are a lot of talented people out there."

Are the creative directories effective? Lee comments, "A directory is your traveling portfolio. The difference between a directory and a self-promotion piece is that, when an art director gets a self-promotion piece through the mail, she's looking at your piece only, whereas in a directory there are hundreds of artists that she flips through.

"The *Black Book* is expensive. I complain about it every year, but it always works for me. It always pays off. I have never lost money in a directory."

Should a beginning illustrator go this route? Lee says, "Be in at least one directory. There are directories that don't cost as much as the *Black Book*, such as *R.S.V.P.*"

© 1989 Jared D. Lee Studio, Inc.

An advertising agency familiar with the work of busy illustrator Jared Lee gave him this print assignment for Viewmaster Video. "They Are What They Watch" was so well received it led to a television commercial. Lee uses the mixed live action/animated spot as part of his animation reel, sent upon request to interested art buyers.

Lee's portfolio cover was picked up from a job done for an ad agency in Boston. Lee recalls, "I had a real ball with it. I was specifically instructed to draw the dorkiest family I could!

"It's very seldom I draw something for myself," Lee tells us. "Some people do a piece of art expressly for their directory ads. I like to use work that's been printed, that's been successful. This illustration always raises an eyebrow and gets a good laugh—I know people like it; it's the perfect piece to put on the cover of the binder. I've also used the illustration in slide presentations and quite a few times in my promotions—it's a really strong statement."

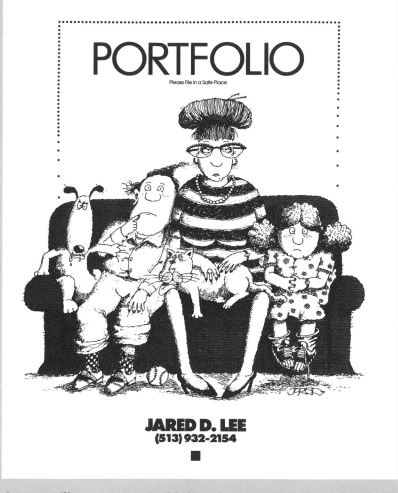

PORTFOLIO
Please File in a Safe Place

JARED D. LEE
(513) 932-2154

Lee also recommends buying a mailing list from brokers—for both beginners and professionals. "You can't beat it. I expect my first mailing list consisted of fifty names. Now it's probably four thousand to five thousand names, and that doesn't include the lists I buy."

Lee's self-promotion isn't restricted to the mail. Traveling to major markets such as New York City or Chicago with prior appointments produces results also. "If I make a trip, it's usually to New York or Chicago. I don't see everybody, but I do see a lot of people. When a response card says, 'Call me the next time you're in the city,' that means the art director wants to see me, so I call him. I also call people who have given me a job in the past. I may take a client I've never met to lunch. I may call an old client just to touch base. While I seldom make cold calls now, that's all there were when I started out. I knocked on a lot of doors."

Lee recommends that artists starting out in their careers do the same, being prepared to take rejection as well as success in stride. "People were very nice to me. You don't want to take it personally when art directors are too busy. It's not easy to see people, even for me. I still hear this from clients: 'Jared, I'm glad you're in town, but I'm swamped.' But I accomplished what I wanted by seeing him, which was to touch base with him. I didn't get to see him, but he said call me the next time, so I'll see him next time. I captured his attention again for five seconds, and when a job comes up, he'll know how to reach me."

A. Give yourself a graphic overhaul. You want to present a unified visual identity. Create a logo to complement a business card, letterhead (stationery imprinted with your name, address, and phone number), plus envelopes. Choose a clean typeface that works with this visual (creating a standard image) and recycle this combination throughout your paperwork. Now, as soon as a potential client sees anything with your name on it, it looks like you mean business. Visualize how good this small, but highly professional touch makes you look when your correspondence hits that art director's desk.

Oh, yes—labels (graphically designed around your logo, name, and address) are very handy, but not vital. If labels are not immediately within budget, simply get a rubber stamp. Printed, personalized billing looks sharp but is not a crucial first concern. You can type (or use pre-printed) invoices (with or without the rubber stamp) until you can afford otherwise.

EXPENSES

Q. *How much will this cost?*

A. If you're complaining that this will cost some money, consider just how polished your competition appears. Establish priorities and do your make-over in baby steps. Use any economical printing means available (as long as you get *good* reproduction), but resolve to present your best face as soon as possible.

Many illustrators budget a certain percentage of their income directly for marketing and self-promotion; a range of 10 percent to 25 percent is common. Illustrator Roger DeMuth jokes that his budget is very clear-cut, "I just spend it until it's gone!"

Estimate a good self-promotional program to cost about $2,000 to $2,500 a year (while not recommended, a quarterly program would run in the neighborhood of $1,000). For some, the thought of spending $1,000 to $2,000 will require immediate CPR. Other illustrators will get a good chuckle from this paltry advertising allowance. These are, in my experience, accurate figures, but, of course, these numbers are not written in stone.

It will become fairly obvious that you're going to have to spend a little money to make a little money. Our $2,500 ceiling starts to look like small change when you investigate the cost of advertising in the creative directories. You could buy a car for the cost of a single page in certain annuals! Conversely, many artists (myself included) have had gratifying responses from spartan reminders economically printed or intentionally prepared as rudimentary photocopies. The trick here is to look funky and fun. As an occasional contrast to those slick, glossy promos, these can be lively and entertaining.

Indiana illustrator Ned Shaw advises, "Don't ever scrimp on your business, even if you have to borrow money from your granny!" Effective marketing and self-promotion can be a substantial investment, but the returns are phenomenal. Whatever you spend should be considered a good investment in yourself, your business, and your future.

PRIORITIES

Q. *What comes first in a self-promotion campaign?*

A. Figuring the brochure would generate business—which generates correspondence—I did my brochure first, then the business cards, and letterhead and envelopes soon after. Labels arrived down the road a bit. I do my invoices on my Macintosh. The computer has been an unparalleled asset—from organizing my mailing list and labels to maintaining my correspondence and generating invoices, to keeping my accounts and writing this book. In addition, because of its graphic capabilities, I've even been able to use the computer as a drawing and design tool on certain assignments.

To save time and expense I design generically. This way, a number of different pieces could be printed simultaneously (thus economically) using the same elements. (You can also cut costs by grouping color separations together.)

Here's a basic recipe for successful self-promotion. Send out a brochure to serve as an introduction and to display your initial samples. This mini-portfolio displays one to four

USING MATERIALS AT HAND

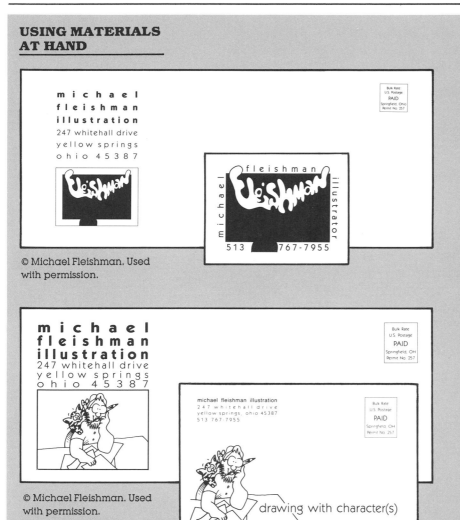

© Michael Fleishman. Used with permission.

© Michael Fleishman. Used with permission.

The author's color logo on his business card was simply scaled down to fit his stationery. It subsequently moves from that page to the envelope without change (with the horizontal letterhead repositioned to fit the envelope format).

He illustrates his black-and-white envelopes by cropping a drawing used on a reminder. He then simply shifts type to create the square mailing label. To insure continuity, the typeface on every mailing is the same; he varies weight and size (as well as jumping from caps to lower case), according to design. On card backs, the return address and mailing indice (the bulk mail info) are a constant. A new drawing (always in the same position to allow for a standard mailing label) is incorporated into the basic shell with every reminder.

examples of your illustration, provides background information, and shows off your style. It should be general enough to cover a lot of territory. You want this mailing to be particularly compelling and to provoke response (hopefully positive).

Towards this end, design the initial brochure to contain a self-returnable postage-paid reply card. This is a convenient way to hear from the people on your list. When you get an affirmative return (either over the phone or through the mail), contact and prepare a submission for that particular client. When the reaction is negative, file accordingly.

Follow the brochure with a promo piece on a regular basis—every thirty to ninety days, as your program dictates and your budget allows. There are artists who blitz art directors with one or two mailings every week or two, which is overkill. If done short-term and to a very limited list, this type of promotion may encourage some art directors to see what all the fuss is about, but you're probably walking a tightrope.

There are many opinions about how often to send mailings. There is the school of thought that says you should send frequent reminders—a monthly or bi-monthly program. Others feel that if you must advertise so much, you are pushing the wrong product. After ninety days a promo cannot really be termed a "reminder," and a quarterly program is ineffective because it allows too much lag time.

I don't think there's any definitive answer (I myself do a mailing every forty-five to sixty days, and it's been extremely effective for me). What I do know is that a *consistent* program is the key.

Systematic reminders, in flyer or postcard form, serve as a continual memorandum of who you are and what you do. Flyers are great and color is lovely, but they aren't feasible on a limited budget if used with regularity. Simple, low-cost postcards in black and white can do the job famously.

Whatever you send, remember that the bottom line is good design coupled with quality reproduction. In *The Graphic Artist's Guide to Marketing and Self-Promotion*, Sally Prince Davis suggests thinking of your brochure (a pamphlet, booklet, or multifold) as a sixty-second commercial, and a flyer (a single sheet, printed one side) as a thirty-second one. Your postcards thus become the fifteen-second spots.

Don't expect an immediate or overwhelming response to any advertising. Be gratified when it happens, but even if it doesn't, keep the program going. Think "crock pot" rather than "microwave." Sometimes the client needs to see more, sometimes the brochure makes a quick sale. Either way the goal is to make sure the markets know you're out there and not let them forget you.

LACK OF PUBLISHED SAMPLES

Q. *When you don't have any published work to show, what do you send as samples?*

A. Give yourself some assignments! Illustrate a magazine article, work up a newspaper advertisement, create a greeting card, illustrate a few pages from a favorite book, design next week's *TV Guide* cover, or compile all your hilarious cartoons in one volume. "Published" work is not the litmus test for a bonafide portfolio of samples. If you are intimidated by your lack of credits, the art director will certainly be loath to hire you. Published credits or no, self-

confidence combined with strong art in a sample package are the best clues that an artist can provide the dynamic images an art director demands.

ORIGINAL WORK AS SAMPLES

Q. *Should original work ever be sent as samples?*

A. Read my lips: Never. As good as the postal services are, things can be lost or damaged when mailed. When you send original work as samples, you run the risk of losing valuable art that can never be replaced. Insurance compensation covers the monetary worth of the art, but the actual piece is gone. Send good quality reproductions: transparencies, stats, tearsheets, photography, or photocopies. Don't take any unnecessary chances with the genuine article.

TEARSHEETS

Q. *What are tearsheets?*

A. Tearsheets are the actual printed pages on which your art appears, "torn" (a euphemism for careful, clean removal) from the binding of an entire publication. Removing the page makes it easier to handle in a client review. Rather than forwarding a bulky magazine or book in a mailed submission, send tearsheets. Instead of utilizing the original in a portfolio, include the tearsheet.

MAILING A PORTFOLIO

Q. *When sending samples to an art director for an introductory look, should you send a portfolio?*

A. Mailing an organized sample presentation can be termed "sending a portfolio" of your work. Do not send the actual binder (nor physical art). Keep in mind that many busy creative service buyers don't care to see unsolicited submissions (a sample package, sent cold, without their request). Send a generic brochure with a reply card first; it's far more effective for all concerned. Have you designated markets on which you intend to really concentrate? In this case, initially target your promotional material to these buyers.

Choose and design around appropriate imagery, then route the advertising to this selected clientele. Say "hello" with your stunning flyer, but let the art director indicate what to do next. Get the necessary feedback and then aim portfolios of particular samples at those interested buyers.

REPRESENTATIVE SAMPLES

Q. *Should you target submissions to a certain company, or should you show representative samples of your work?*

A. Remember—any sample you send should be a representative example of your work. Individualized portfolios will naturally contain kindred illustrations chosen for a certain market or special customer. Save these submissions as the snappy follow up to a strong introduction.

NUMBER OF SAMPLES

Q. *How many samples should I send?*

A. Less is definitely more. Don't pack your portfolio with everything you've done since the third grade. The number varies with everybody you talk to, but a good range is ten to twenty samples of only your absolute best.

SASE

Q. *What is a SASE?*

A. A SASE is a self-addressed, stamped envelope. To insure the return of a posted submission, a SASE should accompany that submission when mailed to a client.

KNOWING WHAT TO SEND

Q. *How do you find out what an art director wants to see in a sample?*

A. Request a sample issue of the magazine. Research an agency's recent advertisements. Talk to other illustrators who've worked with the client. Go to the card shop and browse. Dig through a month's worth of recent newspapers. Call a secretary or an assistant for some advice before you make that submission to the boss—a friendly insider will probably love being approached as the "person in the know,"

and can provide invaluable information regarding the company's art direction. You can always cut right to the chase, of course, and simply ask the art director.

CALLING ART DIRECTORS

Q. *Should you call an art director before you send work?*

A. A call is okay; a query letter is better. Cold calls (unsolicited contacts) are often frustrating and draining for the artist or annoying for the art director. It isn't necessary to call before sending a promo, and it's a bit redundant to call after *every* reminder (although I know this is done by some folks). Enclosing a reply card with your brochure provides initial directions, so it's not essential to use the telephone here either. While persistence is a crucial factor, art directors don't like to be hounded incessantly; timely and consistent self-promotion, helped by a lot of sweat equity (and a spot of luck) will get you inside. But not to shortchange the telephone, a phone call can work magic in any number of instances.

Certainly use the telephone:

- To "formally introduce yourself." This is a nice lead-in to "Would you like to see a portfolio?"
- If you have received a positive response (but no assignment) on a reply card, call to say hello and to express the desire to establish a future relationship. See if you can send your portfolio, or at least a few samples, as the follow up to this introduction.
- When you've received an affirmative return plus a request to forward a portfolio. Great! Call to introduce yourself and to express your delight at the continued opportunity to show more of your work. Send the portfolio right away.
- If you haven't received any response to your mailings, you may want to evaluate your situation through personal contact. Don't badger the client; simply call to update your mailing list. Politely inquire about your mailings and ask if the prospect wishes to receive further

COMBINING TWO CAREERS

Roger DeMuth teaches at Syracuse University while enjoying a flourishing freelance career at the same time. DeMuth maintains, "I wouldn't want to do anything to disrupt the work I do on my own. I get a lot out of it, I have a great time doing it, and I think bringing that experience to my students is very important."

Active both at the drawing board and in the classroom, Roger's first freelance assignments were homegrown. He says, "While attending RIT (in Rochester, New York), a couple of posters I did for faculty member Bob Conge led to some freelance work with him. I worked in Conge's studio a year and a half while I was going to school, and for about six months after graduation. I freelanced with Bob for four or five years after that.

"This was a part-time position. I would do anything from gofer work to picking up stats, from running to the art supply store to lettering posters.

"We did a lot of slide presentations for Eastman Kodak. So I worked on those with him—drawings, inkings, the cut paper, or cell vinyl painting on the back side of the acetates. That was my first commercial work in a studio.

"Eventually I left and hit the road, doing work for a record company that's been a client since 1968. I'm just working on my fourteenth record album with them. I've done all their record bags, record albums, their logos—all of it has been illustrated. It's been a nice relationship."

What is DeMuth's advice for beginning freelancers? He tells us,"Starting out, you don't have much money. There are very

few ways to get national exposure, except through the competitions like American Illustration or the Society of Illustrators. This is a little risky in the beginning—you really can't count on it. If it happens, that's great. If you want national work, it seems you have to either advertise in the national publications like *American Showcase* or do impressive mailings.

"Those things take a lot of time, so I think it's best to build up experience at a local level. Work with people who are right near you. You can go back and forth. There's a little give and take there. You can see the expression on their faces when you turn something in and they don't like it—or if they do like it, you get the compliment immediately. It's very important to know if someone likes your work or doesn't like it. And you learn something from that relationship.

"Working in a studio is good experience, seeing different aspects of the business. Whatever you can do to get your foot in the door is a step in the right direction. I see a lot of students that don't wait for graduation. I think that's a good idea. While going to school, try doing some freelance work in a studio, or an internship of some sort. You need that in lieu of the big bucks right now. You need some work experience at a student level.

"It's difficult to freelance right out of school. Have a part-time job lined up. Things will go a little smoother. There are many things that have to be done: Chromes of your work—4"x5" or 8"x10"—are very expensive; you need a promotional piece that should be printed, and those things are several hundred dollars at a minimum.

"You can certainly freelance some of it. The nature of freelance is that it doesn't have to be full-time, it can be what you want to make it. Anyone can call himself a freelancer—from someone who does one job a year, or one job in their lifetime—so it's really what you want out of it. If your work is good enough, saleable enough, choose your own hours. It all depends on the individual."

As both an illustration professional and an educator, DeMuth has some words of wisdom regarding that all-important portfolio. "Select ten to fifteen of your best pieces. It's difficult to choose the best pieces, so you'll need a little bit of advice.

This illustration was in *American Illustration*, the Society of Illustrators show, and won an award from the Rochester Society of Communication Arts. It has also appeared in Korea's *Design Journal* as part of an article about Roger DeMuth's work. Mailed as a promo and used in sample packets, the image is a compilation of basement "horror" stories, real and imagined. Done "just for fun," the illustration has garnered DeMuth tremendous exposure.

Show your portfolio to a few people and get some feedback—sometimes artists are too close to their work. A second opinion doesn't hurt. Take it to an art director, or someone close, someone at a school, even a family member. I get advice from my wife occasionally, and she'll say something that's very honest. I'll get uppity sometimes, and then twenty minutes later I'll say, 'You know, she's right.' Put things in piles—this is one style of work, this is another style, this is stronger than that. Try to make judgments. You don't want many, many pieces in a portfolio.

"It certainly seems that people are more specialized now than they used to be. If you're in New York or in a large city and starting out, art directors get confused if they see too many styles going on in a portfolio. New York is a city of specialists and very specialized styles of illustration. In the New York area, you need a different portfolio than you would for a small city (where you'd be called upon to do a wider variety of styles).

"However, you can still have a range of styles. Each person has an idea of what they'd like to do from the images they've put into their portfolio. The people who do the best, though, are those with a specific goal in mind—like working for a newspaper or doing editorial illustrations. It helps to have a direction in which you want to go."

How important is self-promotion? "*Very* important," says DeMuth. "You have to let people know of your newest work. You need to let them know you're still alive, but don't bug them. Be gentle and hope for the best.

"Even students need some kind of promotional piece right in the beginning—something with your name, address, and telephone number, plus several images. Just a card with your work is enough—rubber stamp your name on the back.

"I think a postcard is a good format, because a lot of art directors are inundated with promotional material. A postcard is fairly inexpensive to produce. Somewhere between one and three images on a postcard gives someone a good idea of what you do."

As a side note, DeMuth advises, "I wouldn't recommend beginners calling art directors. I think sending them that postcard is plenty. Mailing a package of samples or dropping off a portfolio is fine. I don't think the phone call is going to make the sale in the beginning. If they like your work, they'll call you."

From his vantage point of twenty years in the illustration business, DeMuth capsulizes the freelance process this way, "You must first produce good quality work. Then you have to get rid of that work—advertise it somehow, so there's that promotional type of effort. Then you wait for the phone to ring, then you have to do these jobs that come in.

"The promotion is very important, the promotional piece is very important, and producing good work is very important. Everything seems to be working into a full-time job. You can do all of these things, but it takes time away from your artwork. It's almost a full-time job maintaining a mailing list! It's a real struggle. I think my work is better than it's ever been—I'm very pleased with what I'm doing—but it's still very difficult to do good work."

Has the business changed for DeMuth over time? "I haven't shown my portfolio in years," he says. "Although I meet with people—I show them a few things, bring a couple of samples, or my sketchbook—but I don't make an appointment to go out and show my work anymore, and that's a little different than it used to be.

"The advent of fax machines has changed things around." He adds, "I have letters from art directors dating back fifteen years ago that say, 'If you want to work in New York, you have to live in New York.' That's not the case any longer. I may not be next door, so I can't go out to lunch with them. I can't run over and talk or just stop by and say hello (which sometimes is very nice), but I advertise, and my fax machine works very well."

Summing up, Roger says, "In the beginning, you need to experiment in all different areas. I wasn't just an illustrator, I wasn't just a designer; I did all of these things and more. You really don't want to exclude things. If it's an opportunity, take it. It's worked pretty well for me!"

In this card DeMuth's hungry canine unfolds to become an even hungrier alligator. DeMuth's promos play an important part in his marketing strategy.

samples. Say something like, "I've been sending my promotional material for some time and I just wanted to personally say hello. I'm updating my program now—can I keep you on my mailing list? Thanks. Look for something exciting in the mail soon."

- To expedite the response to a mailed submission in limbo. What is happening with that portfolio sent back in March? Don't harangue; say how eager you are to do business and pleasantly request the status of that submission.

Personal contact has definite benefits. All of a sudden you're a real person, talking to another real person on the other end of the line. Behind the scrawled signature, beyond print, there's an actual voice and a genuine personality at which the paperwork only hints. A phone call carries a tone of immediate persuasion, while written correspondence may not. Don't hesitate to use the phone; it can be to your distinct advantage.

SIMULTANEOUS SUBMISSIONS

Q. *Is it a good idea to send simultaneous submissions?*

A. There's no reason to sit and wait for the return of a submission—or even a reaction to that material—before sending it on to another client. Regardless of how prompt the response, you'll find that there'll be way too much lag time between your submission and a buyer's reply to warrant exclusivity.

COMPILING A MAILING LIST

Q. *How do you compile a mailing list? Do you use the names of personal contacts only, or do you find names in directories?*

A. When starting out, personal contacts (if and when you have them) should be a part of that list. However, you'll probably find the number of these clients insufficient for your total mailing needs. Your mailing list needs to be a comprehensive one.

The phone book is a good place to look, but, while a great local source, listings won't be complete. The best directory to use to find new

clients is *Artist's Market*, published yearly by Writer's Digest Books. *Artist's Market* is the complete "where and how to sell your graphic art" directory. With over 2,500 listings, it includes contact names, addresses, pay rates, and buyer's needs, while detailing submission requirements and tips from the buyers themselves. The most recent edition is usually available each year around September.

You can always find *Artist's Market*, plus numerous other directories, at your local library. You can buy the directories—but many of these volumes are expensive and not readily available. If your budget is currently limited, spend some time in the library's reference section and bring change for the photocopier.

RENTING MAILING LISTS

Q. *Should you rent lists from list brokers?*

A. I would advise investigating a list broker, but only if it's within your means. List brokers are a good source for contacts. Do your homework—the costs of obtaining their lists vary, plus they usually charge for a one-time use (and some are more stringent than others).

Obviously, it could get expensive if you're reusing the list, but New York illustrator Kathie Abrams tells us, "If you pick up a list rental with phone numbers, you can make follow-up calls. Once you have contacted an art director, you have captured that name and can mail to her again." Also, make sure to get a printout to keep. If you get only labels, they go out on the mailing and you won't know who you mailed to or what their phone number is.

Illustrator Peter Spacek tells us, "You'll be surprised at the places you'll get work from—places you'd never think of sending samples or taking your book. So buy a big list from a known list broker and go for it. It'll pay off."

ARTIST REPS

Q. *Does a beginner need a rep?*

A. Many illustrators swear by artist's representatives; many swear at them. There are some agents who take full credit for the success of their clients (as if the creative's talent and skill hardly matter), and there are those artists who feel they're every bit the super sales and service force a good rep can be.

Illustrator Roger T. DeMuth has two reps (in Rochester and Boston). He says, "To get a rep, you almost have to not need one. When your work is saleable, you get a rep. They usually want to rep you when you don't need them!" Illustrator Ned Shaw adds, "If a rep is really hot, they only take big money earners. Only work with a rep if they are better at selling than you are."

Illustrator Fred Carlson, in his article, "Marketing Illustration in the National Arena," (published in the Graphic Artist's Guild at-large newsletter) asks these key questions: "Is the 25 to 30 percent commission worth it in terms of your return on any assignment? Can a third party describe your work with the clarity that you can yourself? Can you trust this third party to receive the check and pass on your 70 to 75 percent due at once? And finally, will this third party work as hard in your best interests as you would yourself?"

Can a beginning illustrator get a rep? Realistically, probably not. An untested novice, you're too green—and quite a risky gamble at this early stage of your game. This is not to say that it's absolutely impossible.

Some newcomers seem to hit the streets running. Boasting unmistakeable ability and oozing fresh technique, they are in the right place at the right time. In this story, Cinderella's creative approach counterbalances her tender experience, and she offers a style ripe for the current needs of a ready marketplace. Agents are always looking for these audacious talents; it's a sweet fairy tale, but it is not the industry norm.

Do you need a rep? Maybe. Illustrator Benton Mahan believes, "Most people, especially in the beginning, can be their own best agent."

CHAPTER THREE CHECKLISTS

What is self-promotion?
☐ Blowing your own horn.
☐ Letting people know who you are, what you do, and reminding them.
☐ Investing in your business with quality printed samples.
☐ Making sure that the right people see that work.
☐ Good graphics do not have to be expensive or four color.
☐ A promo reproduced on a high quality photocopier can look good and be cost effective.
☐ Explore the new color photocopiers.
☐ Study your mailing list and determine what you'll be sending, the sequence of events, and when; tally the number of pieces you need.
☐ Hire a typesetter and printer, or locate a quick print center; if you're a colorist you'll need a color separator or color photocopier.

Give yourself a graphic overhaul by:
☐ Redoing your logo for your business card, letterhead, and envelopes.
☐ Choosing a clean typeface that works with your new image.
☐ Considering a word processor for mailing list and labels, correspondence, invoices, and bookkeeping.
☐ Designing generically; print a number of pieces simultaneously and thus economically.

Steps to successful self-promotion:
☐ Send out a brochure to serve as an introduction and to display your initial samples. Design the initial brochure to contain a self-returnable postage-paid reply card.
☐ When you get an affirmative return, contact that particular client and prepare a submission. When the reaction is negative, file accordingly.

HOW DO YOU GET NOTICED? **43**

☐ Follow the brochure with a promo piece on a regular basis, about every thirty to ninety days.

☐ Don't expect an immediate or over-whelming response.

☐ Estimate a good self-promotional program to cost about $2,000 to $2,500 a year; a quarterly program would run in the neighborhood of $1,000.

When there is no published work to show, give yourself some assignments, such as:

☐ Illustrating an existing magazine article.

☐ Working up a newspaper advertisement

☐ Creating a greeting card.

☐ Drawing a few pages from a favorite book.

☐ Designing next week's *TV Guide* cover.

☐ Compiling all your hilarious cartoons in one volume.

When sending samples for an introductory look:

☐ Send reproductions or a generic brochure with a reply card. Don't send the actual binder or original art.

☐ Target your promotional material to certain buyers; choose and design around appropriate imagery, then route the advertising to this selected clientele.

☐ Let the art director indicate what to do next; get feedback, *then* aim portfolios of particular samples at the request of interested buyers.

☐ Send individualized portfolios as the snappy follow up to a strong introduction.

How to determine what art directors want to see in a sample package:

☐ Request a sample issue of the magazine.

☐ Research an agency's recent advertisements.

☐ Talk to other illustrators who've worked with a publisher.

☐ Go to the card shop or newsstand and browse.

☐ Dig through a month's worth of recent newspapers.

☐ Call a secretary or an assistant for some advice.

☐ Phone to ask the art director.

To contact an art director:

☐ Send a query letter first.

☐ It's not necessary to call before sending a promo.

☐ It's redundant to call after every reminder.

☐ Enclose a reply card with your brochure.

☐ Persistence pays off, but don't hound.

Use the telephone:

☐ To formally introduce yourself.

☐ If you have received a positive response (but no assignment) on a reply card.

☐ When you've received an affirmative return plus a request to forward a portfolio.

☐ If you haven't received any response to your mailings.

☐ To expedite the response to a mailed submission in limbo.

How to compile a mailing list:

☐ List personal contacts.

☐ Use the phone book to look up local ad agencies, studios, etc.

☐ Consult *Artist's Market* or other directories.

☐ Rent names from a list broker.

CHAPTER 4
WHAT GOES INTO A PORTFOLIO?

DEFINING A PORTFOLIO

Q. *What is a portfolio?*

A. A portfolio is a collected display of samples. It's a planned presentation of your work, used to communicate your abilities to a potential client.

PORTFOLIO REVIEW

Q. *What happens during a portfolio review? Is it just like a job interview?*

A. Generally, portfolio reviews are less formal than job interviews, but the game rules don't vary much. What counts is self-confidence, a positive attitude, and good personal appearance. You don't have to wear a suit, but dress fashionably and neatly.

If you're right-handed, carry your portfolio in your left; be ready to shake hands with the art director without fumbling or shifting the binder. (If you're left-handed, carry your portfolio in your left hand, also.) Eye contact is also a sign of confidence. Look your client square in the face, open your book, and knock some socks off!

INVESTING IN A PORTFOLIO

Q. *Since I'm just starting out as a freelancer, should I invest a lot in my portfolio?*

A. It's only your career we're talking about here, so as illustrator Mary Grace Eubank advises, "Invest whatever it takes to represent your work at its very finest. You can look like a million dollars while flaunting credits and scholastic achievements like crazy, but ultimately it is your portfolio that will make—or break—your chances."

SIZE OF A PORTFOLIO

Q. *Does the actual size of a portfolio matter? Is big better?*

A. Don't sacrifice quality for quantity, and big is not necessarily better. A compact, manageable portfolio with ten to twenty pieces makes for an easier, smoother presentation. Bulky binders are heavy and unwieldy. At best, you'll just look clumsy flailing these free weights around the art director's desk. A portfolio review should be a visual workout, not physical exercise for the art director.

Matting each piece is an option (if done with skill), but this may only add weight. Protect your work by mounting your samples in acetate, polyester, or vinyl sleeves. Think about mounting and laminating loose tearsheets not presented within a sleeve. Lamination adds expense, but looks great and will preserve the life of each piece.

Mounting your work on a black background looks professional and won't distract from your piece (remember, you're selling the art, not the frame). Some artists mount on white, but I feel a white (even off-white) sheet is too bright and glossy—I want the piece to shine, not the backdrop. However, if your samples are dark and broody, a white backing may provide the proper contrast.

Nothing will disguise mediocre work. Despite the gimmicks, a high-tech binder with space program technology and technicolor sleeves won't cut it. Substance, not flash, makes the sale.

MAILING PORTFOLIOS

Q. *Do you ever mail portfolios? How do you protect them?*

A. In that a "portfolio" is an organized presentation of your illustration, you may find yourself mailing a portfolio to prospective clients.

You won't be forwarding the actual binder containing those irreplaceable originals or tearsheets. You will be mailing compiled reproductions—extra tearsheets, C-prints (a full-color positive print from a negative transparency), photostats (produced by photographic process with paper negatives), high-quality photocopies, photography, or transparencies.

The best alternative to flat work would be a slide portfolio (slides are also called transparencies). Prepare one sleeve of no more than twenty 35mm slides (the larger formats are fine, but 35mm is most convenient). Label each slide *and* the sleeve, and enclose a self-addressed, postage-paid envelope for their safe return. Slides are an easy, practical solution for both you and a busy art director.

When mailing, you'll need to virtually "bulletproof" your submission—you want your package to arrive undamaged, and much can happen during the round trip between postboxes.

Present all samples inside a folder and sandwich this between two pieces of cardboard, matt board, styrofoam, or foam core. (You should also protect an art assignment you're mailing by placing it under tissue and between two pieces of card, hinged by tape.) Label the folder and individual pieces. Be sure to enclose a cover letter and your business card. Of course, completely label the outside packaging.

The outer wrap may be a manila or foam-padded envelope, bubble wrap, or even brown wrapping paper. Or you could insert the infrastructure between two additional pieces of cardboard, rather than using an envelope. This will further safeguard the package.

Use package sealing tape (masking tape is frowned upon by the post office and many airfreight services) or reinforced tape, if you're really cautious. On the front of the package, write or stamp "PLEASE DO NOT BEND OR FOLD— ARTWORK ENCLOSED." Include an SASE for the return of your material.

ARRANGING A PORTFOLIO REVIEW

Q. *Is it better to call or write to schedule a portfolio review?*

A. Requesting and scheduling a portfolio review are, of course, two different things. Scheduling hinges on an affirmative answer to a request, and either can be done by letter or telephone.

A phone request is informal (even intimate)—quick and right to the point. The written request can be backed by visuals—after all, you're selling product, not patter. Neither method has a definite edge, so take some thought to determine how you want to communicate with the art director.

Some folks are natural writers; their polished letters are powerful and persuasive. Others prefer the immediate and individual interaction only the telephone provides. As you'll be spending lots of time on the phone and at the keyboard (business generates correspondence and vice versa), you'll have plenty of opportunities to develop your communication skills.

COLD CALLS

Q. *What is a cold call?*

A. A cold call is a contact without request or referral. It can get you a portfolio review without the preliminary wait involved with written correspondence. Cold calls require time and energy you may not want to expend. It is essentially selling door to door, and it can be frustrating.

For some illustrators the very idea of the cold call is unthinkable; others hate them, but still call as a simple matter of fact. Many illustrators thrive on the practice, viewing cold calls as just another avenue for pursuing yet more business. It's a sure way to test your tolerance for rejection, but a good salesman can get a good return for the trouble.

DROP-OFF POLICY

Q. *What is a "drop-off" policy?*

A. Many busy art directors will only look at portfolios at specific hours on certain days. Still others require that the illustrator leave ("drop-off") the portfolio, then pick it up later at a scheduled date or time. There's usually a written reaction with your "book" (another term for portfolio), possibly a critique or suggestions. If the art director is interested, an appointment is arranged.

Yes, you read right; you won't be there. If you feel your portfolio is not strong enough to 'speak' for you in your absence, don't show it yet. Take some time and get that book in shape.

Many artists find that the drop-off saves time and eliminates uninterested prospects. Eventually you'll face a drop-off policy. It's quite a common practice (and nothing unusual) when making rounds in a larger market—in fact, it seems that the drop-off policy is simply standard operating procedure in New York City these days.

At some point you'll have to decide how you feel about leaving your book and the inherent dangers and benefits thereof. Before the portfolio ever leaves your hands, consider how to minimize any risks involved. Expendable samples (tearsheets, stats, promo pieces, photography, transparencies) will hopscotch the considerable pain of lost originals. A strong binder and sturdy presentation will buffet the blows the portfolio will weather in its travels. Protect the samples under acetate, making sure they're securely mounted. Label clearly and completely. Have someone sign for the portfolio before you leave the office.

Finally, fight your paranoia. These strangers ("doing who knows what with my precious watercolors") are the same wonderful folks with the choice assignments. A healthy attitude will be awarded by a sigh of relief when the portfolio is safely back in your possession. And guess what? You landed an assignment!

TARGETING A PORTFOLIO

Q. *Should I change my portfolio for each type of market I show it to?*

A. Many artists, like Mary Grace Eubank, work in concentrated markets. Eubank says she cannot relate to changing her portfolio; "I started doing giftwrap, then went into greeting cards, and from there I went into children's books." Even though she's worked in many markets, she keeps her portfolio the same (but updated).

If you have many pieces from which to pick and choose, orient your portfolio to particular markets; a binder with interchangeable sleeves can facilitate this process. At the beginning, you may not have many pieces from various markets. This means a somewhat generic portfolio that addresses a wider client base— not a sampling of divergent styles, but a portfolio that meets a variety of needs.

Although a quirky line style reproduces well and is strong and compelling, the folks at a card company won't relate to a portfolio of

SEVEN LAWS OF SUBMITTING WORK THROUGH THE MAIL

1. Submit work to the appropriate person.

2. Send your portfolio when you say you will.

3. Samples must be organized, neatly presented, clearly labeled, expendable, and focused.

4. Write a personal cover letter on your letterhead. Make it brief and friendly—not too proud, not too humble. Include a self-addressed, stamped envelope for the return of the samples. Realize that you won't get your work back immediately—it is being viewed by any number of busy people with hectic schedules.

5. Follow up with a card or phone call. Follow that phone call with another. Remember, with all the hustle and bustle, art directors need your help to connect your name with your artwork. Do not give up, but don't be pushy. When it becomes necessary to inquire about the status of your portfolio, be absolutely courteous.

6. Send new samples frequently. Remind the art director of the valuable contribution you are anxious to make. You want your card on their bulletin board.

7. Build your list of contact names to create more opportunities.

black-and-white editorial samples. If you add color and gags (and present card mock-ups), the art director can visualize how to use your work. By the same token, greeting cards would not go over at advertising agencies. The imagery you show must be in the context of an ad (with type) to show how your work meets the agency's needs.

Sometimes different markets overlap, but people will tend to classify your work. It's a little tough to break barriers and preconceived ideas. The rule of thumb is to always show what's relevant.

MAKING YOUR OWN
BOOK A GOOD READ

New York City illustrator Kathie Abrams doesn't remember her first assignment. A freelancer since 1978, Abrams says, "In the first year or two, I did a number of illustrations for *Sing Out!*, a now-defunct folksong journal—all freebies. I was pretty uninformed at the beginning, so much so that I wonder whether I was deliberately keeping a lot of information out. It's not hard to figure out how to approach this business—it's just hard to get out and do it! What a relief it was to finally get assignments," she sighs. "There's nothing like good honest work to cure neurosis."

Abrams' college background was in art history, with a studio major. She didn't find work immediately as an illustrator after college. "I worked for two years in children's book publishing as a 'reader'—I read books all day—before I went back to Parsons for two years of illustration training." Not coincidentally, Abrams' first breaks were in children's books, a field with which she was familiar.

Abrams freelanced right after art school. "I was rather vague and dreamy about what being an illustrator meant," she says. "I think it might have been helpful if I had had more staff experience. It is important to understand how our business works, why art directors choose a certain illustrator, what clients are like, and how production works. I did have publishing experience, and had friends in the children's book field, but I knew very little about magazines or advertising."

But Abrams learned well. Picking up great credentials, she shares this considerable expertise as a teacher of illustration at the Moore College of Art.

As part of her class load, Abrams teaches a portfolio course. She believes art directors are looking for good thinkers when they review a portfolio. "Art buyers will be concentrating on your style and your subject matter," she says, "and if your book includes something similar to the assignments that cross his desk. Research the field. Show that you can do similar work."

What *does* go into a portfolio? Abrams replies, "The fast answer is 'twelve to fifteen examples of your finest work,' and its corollary 'eight great pieces are better than twenty mediocre ones.' These axioms are probably still the best replies.

"A portfolio is like a picture book. A pace is created as you flip the pages, so get an effect you like. Try it out in different ways. Leaf through the book until you feel it is really consistent. It can be dramatic, all punches. It can be cozy and intimate. It can be slick and technically dazzling. You can work up to a punch and then ease off, or each page can be on its own with no sense of 'story line.' "

Abrams feels that to achieve the greatest artistic satisfaction an illustrator must start with the art she naturally creates—her own best subjects and style.

"Portfolios may need to be changed for different markets, but if you have fifteen swell pieces that pace nicely and give you pleasure when you look at them, show them around a bit before you start shuffling.

"See what markets are 'naturals' for you. You can't cover all the bases and be in everyone's office at the right time."

What about format? "The portfolio itself should stay out of the way of your art," states Abrams. "If it quietly and efficiently showcases your work, it's doing its job. I usually show one piece of art on a page. There's another school of thought that feels showing a great deal of work promotes respectability; people get work using both approaches.

"If you're just starting out, don't spend a million bucks," Abrams recommends. "But you may have to spend a few hundred."

She also issues these words of caution, "If you can't live without the original work in your portfolio, don't leave it! In order to have a book you can drop-off overnight, you may have to make transparencies, color prints, slides, or stats. You should also leave a promo with your name and phone number on it to remind the art director why she wants to reach you.

About the actual binder, Abrams tells us, "I've used a big portfolio—a museum box-type affair measuring about 16" × 18" and weighing a ton. I used it for two years—my back went out twice—because I really wanted to make an impression and be able to show spreads. It went over quite well, but I'm much happier with my 11" × 14" box.

Portfolios measuring 18" × 24" seem awfully big when you get them in an art director's office and try to lay them out on the desk. A few people personally presenting large oil paintings probably still need them, but I'd take art directors seriously if they start saying 'Have you thought about getting 8" × 10" transparencies of these?' "

Once you get into the art director's office, Abrams offers this advice, "I didn't believe it until I saw it, but it's a fact that many art directors can look at your portfolio in thirty seconds flat—and be aware of what they saw. If that happens to you, don't be insulted. Find out whether they'd like to be kept on your mailing list. When you have a substantial amount of new work, go see them again. If you're not right for their needs, maybe they know someone else whom you should see.

"The bottom line is that your portfolio should reflect you. You are looking to connect with those art buyers who are on your wavelength. Not everyone will be, but there is someone for every style and taste.

"Your goal should be to represent yourself as clearly and attractively as possible so that you can get a response from other people who think the same way you do. I think it is a neurotic experience to try to be everything to everyone."

Summing up, Abrams says, "Most of the illustrators I know are happy, but still feel they must hustle. It's almost impossible to keep on top of the whole field. You end up choosing that part of it you most enjoy. Throughout their careers, most people change directions dramatically or gently make small stylistic changes that open up new markets.

"Beginning freelancers should allow themselves some time to 'catch on'— maybe several years before all their income will come from freelancing. There's no ceiling to what you can earn, but there's no floor, either!"

© Kathie Abrams. Used with permission.

Kathie Abrams' promo from a 1987 *American Showcase* was done in consultation with her rep. The images were handpicked to appeal to advertising agencies. Two components on the page—the "martini man" (bottom right) and "Celebrate"— are actually repeats; response was so great to these pieces, Abrams ran them again.

Abrams uses this *Showcase* page as part of sample packets forwarded to in-terested contacts. While these packages are sent upon request, Abrams prefers to send postcards when doing her seasonal bulk mailings. The perforated and folded cards are easier to ship, cost effective, and a handy size for bulletin boards. The top half carries a visual; the bottom half is a self-returnable reply card. While the image will vary, the basic shell of information never changes from card to card.

ASSEMBLING A PORTFOLIO

Q. *What's the best way to assemble a portfolio? What do I put in it? Should I put my best pieces first?*

A. Repeat these three words while putting the portfolio together: "Only my best." Generally, small is better and less is more. Think in the neighborhood of ten to twenty pieces; don't pack it with everything you've done since the third grade. Focus. Be highly selective. If in doubt about a particular piece, don't use it!

Nothing less than your best work should be in your binder. You're only as strong as your weakest sample. That one inferior piece sandwiched somewhere in the middle of your book will be remembered first—it will detract from the "good stuff" and diminish the impact of the entire portfolio. Don't include anything of which you're not proud. Don't include any style or technique you don't really want to do.

As you develop, so will your portfolio (we're still talking quality, not quantity). A portfolio should never be stagnant—update it regularly. Samples must be well protected, but portable, and easy to change and examine. Make it simple to carry (with or without handle), of uniform page size, and lightweight. A leather or leather-like ring binder (open or zippered) enclosing the transparent sleeves offers the simplest answer here.

There is no distinct advantage to either a vertical or horizontal layout, but your portfolio should not be a lazy Susan; make sure the art director isn't swiveling your book—or his head—around from page to page. Have one consistent page orientation throughout (if this proves impossible, group all horizontal pieces in one section and vertical samples in another. This way the art director only cranes his neck once).

It's a given that neatness is crucial, and that a portfolio must contain crisp, clean samples wrapped in a professional package, all presented with style and taste. A portfolio cannot be a haphazard affair. There should be a planned arrangement and logical progression to the sequence of samples. While good organization is a must, I don't necessarily subscribe to the train of thought that says one must lump all color pieces together (and the same with black-and-white pieces).

The portfolio should be clearly—but tastefully—labeled (no neon lights, just complete identification inside and out). Your work is highly suspect if the presentation shines brighter than your samples.

You can approach the pace and flow of the portfolio in a variety of ways. Chronological (or reverse chronological) organization shows progression and development. Organization by subject matter (for instance, animals, crowd scenes, portraits) works for many artists. You could take a graphic approach and group by technique (such as pen and ink followed by watercolors). You might want to organize thematically and demonstrate problem-solving within a specific body of assignments (advertisements, greeting cards, book jackets).

Always start big and end strong. After the trenchant beginning, some portfolios will build to an exciting finish. Many books crest in the middle and slope to a big bang. Others are like a roller coaster ride—with many visual peaks and rests culminating in a stunning climax.

LABELING PORTFOLIO PIECES

Q. *Does the artist explain each piece in a portfolio, or do you write a note for each piece explaining the work?*

A. Let your work sell itself. Labels can be used as efficient identifiers or as elements of page design. These compositional devices can be effective if used sparingly and with purpose; a brief description noting the title, client, and project is entirely appropriate. If you must write a note detailing each piece, your samples do not pack the visual wallop needed to carry the portfolio.

PRESENTING STYLE IN A PORTFOLIO

Q. *Should you present yourself as a generalist or a specialist in your portfolio?*

A. At the beginning of your career it's best to present a solid, consistent style, especially when selling in the national marketplace.

HIGH-CONTRAST EXPOSURE

Chris Spollen of Staten Island, New York, calls his studio Moonlight Press, and has dubbed his work High Contrast Illustration.

Spollen received his first freelance assignment, from *Crawdaddy* magazine, during his last year of college. The magazine was located across the street from school, and the art director knew some of the graduating seniors. "The job was for a black-and-white spread, plus a spot. It was wonderful. I actually had a printed tearsheet before I even graduated."

At the beginning, Spollen found freelancing to be rough. "It was all local business. I'd hop a bus here in the city, knock on people's doors. The phones are ringing, an art director's tired, they don't want to see you. You have to get a tough skin. I stayed at home until I was twenty-seven years old, went to the city every day, trying to break into the spot illustration market.

"At school, I specialized in illustration and majored in printmaking, so I actually had a complete print portfolio—all hand-colored etchings—primarily fantasy stuff. My fundamental flaw was that I had no concept of my marketplace. I had a very ambitious portfolio that was pointed in the wrong direction."

Spollen says the biggest problem for most beginners is showing a student portfolio. "They put together a portfolio that reflects every teacher they've ever had. Every page looks different. You'll need a portfolio that reflects your strong suit, and for this you have to know yourself. Are you linear? Are you tonal? Do you paint? Do you do pen and ink?

"Concentrate on whatever it is you enjoy, but stay aware of what the art directors are buying. This is essential. Find the illus-

trators' annuals and take a look at who's buying what. Get an idea of the paperback market, the editorial market. Buy magazines. Develop a persepective; be conscious of how your work fits the needs of the marketplace. Once all this is established, then you want twelve pieces—roughly twelve to fourteen—that demonstrate your creative process.

"You have to convey to the art director a consistency of ideas and techniques—your style. The art director wants to pigeonhole you; make it easy for him. If I had it to do over again, I would probably emphasize consistency of a particular technique.

"You have to convince an art director that she needs you. Your best shot is to start small. Little idea-oriented concepts that translate into quarter-page, half-page illustrations will be a foot in the door. Try to get tearsheets as soon as possible (and always negotiate for extra tearsheets to mail out to the people you've already seen). After you've built this portfolio, you can move on to more ambitious pieces."

Spollen thinks networking can help, but says, "Try to live at home as long as you can. A lot of my friends made the same mistake—they graduated from college and got part-time jobs. This is kind of the kiss of death. The field is so competitive and other work takes so much out of you. If your parents are willing and able to subsidize you, take full advantage of this wonderful opportunity and give your career 100 percent."

How about people skills? Spollen maintains, "You have to know people. You have to be able to read them a little bit. I think phone skills are important, too. As in any business, a certain amount of social awareness and decorum obviously can't hurt you.

"While I hated making calls—absolutely hated it with a passion—I always found it easy to talk to art directors. I went door-to-door and drank coffee with them, and then found that to be needless. I made friends, but in a sense reduced myself to a happy-go-lucky messenger.

"About the middle point in my career, I realized it'd be to my advantage to spend more time drawing and less time going door-to-door. With the advent of Federal Express, of course, everything started to change for the better. Now I don't see art directors at all."

A California design firm found Spollen's page in *American Showcase* and gave him this assignment for San Diego Gas and Electric. He was given the topic of "Energy and a New Light," paid a "tremendous fee," and granted total creative freedom. Spollen's powerful contribution to the campaign was selected for a Society of Illustrators annual show. He regards the 1989 illustration as a full-blown culmination of his efforts to date. "It really shows how far you can go with enough tenacity and your wits about you," Spollen remarks, "even if you get off to a rough start."

© Chris Spollen. Used with permission.

And self-promotion? "My self-promotion was very simple. I went to the most immediate form of reproduction possible, and that was offset printing. On graduation, I had two black-and-white offset cards done and I left those with each art director. I would also leave whatever tearsheets I could get my hands on. That was combined with periodic mailings of postcards, and as money became available, I went to a postcard format. Again, I was giving these postcards out—hand addressing, stuffing, and stamping envelopes, then mailing them.

"The big difference—seventeen years later—is basically, I have money now. I simply buy into the leading directories while sending mailers out periodically, probably every three months.

"I would advise anyone starting out to spare themselves a lot of the aggravation I went through. If their parents can give them a little money, go into the directories early on, rather than doing the sporadic mailing. I think you get better exposure if you buy a page in one of the books (which are, in turn, distributed by publishers), rather than trying to distribute cards on your own. I'm positive the directories will serve you better.

"Between what the book and the mailers bring in, I do quite well. I've developed a mailing list. Each time the phone rings, I write down the party's name and address. We send out mailers, and the forms and labels from each mailing are copied and then put onto a master list. We're now up to about six hundred names of people who are familiar with my work or who have made inquiries.

"The bottom line is: If you really want to do this, you'll jump any obstacles. If you want to get married and have a family and think of illustration as a 'nice career'—reconsider. In the beginning there's virtually no return; just a lot of sweat equity and the idea that, at the end of the road, you're going to have this 'nice career' and enjoy it. This pulls you through.

"If you're looking for an immediate, steady income, I'd say illustration is a tough gig. You never know from day to day who you'll be working for, what you're going to be creating next. But a freelance illustration career is also extremely rewarding, satisfying and exciting. It's a delicate balance, but you're never bored. That's the hook of it. It's just totally captivating. I think the positives outweigh the negatives."

CHAPTER FOUR
CHECKLISTS

To maximize the effectiveness of your portfolio, make sure it:
☐ Is compact and manageable for a smooth presentation.
☐ Represents only your best work.
☐ Focuses on a style or technique you want to sell.
☐ Shows about ten to twenty pieces.
☐ Is arranged in a logical progression.
☐ Starts big and ends strong.
☐ Has a consistent page orientation.

Your portfolio can be arranged by:
☐ Subject matter.
☐ Technique.
☐ Theme.
☐ Chronology.

During a portfolio review, you need to:
☐ Show self-confidence and a positive attitude.
☐ Present a neat personal appearance.
☐ Talk to the art director at first to get acquainted.
☐ Let your samples do the talking.

To mail and protect portfolios:
☐ Don't forward the actual binder.
☐ Mail reproductions.
☐ Have a copy of any sample on file — likewise with roughs or comps.
☐ Present all samples inside a folder; sandwich this between two pieces of cardboard, matt board, styrofoam, or foam core.

☐ Label the folder and all individual pieces completely; label the outside with your name and contact information.
☐ Enclose your business card on the inside.
☐ The outer wrap may be a manilla envelope, a foam-padded envelope, bubble wrap, or even brown wrapping paper.
☐ Use package sealing tape or reinforced tape to seal the package.
☐ Write or stamp "PLEASE DO NOT BEND OR FOLD – ARTWORK ENCLOSED" on the front of the package, and include an SASE.

Samples must be:
☐ Clean, crisp, and of high quality; there should be no dog-eared tearsheets, fuzzy photocopies, or mutilated transparencies.
☐ Clearly labeled with your name, address, and phone number; buy a stamp to facilitate this process.
☐ Manageable size for easy viewing.
☐ Neatly presented in an accessible format.
☐ Focused — if a publication uses only black-and-white work, send just that; if a publication uses thoughtful editorial art, do not send trendy commercial art.
☐ Expendable — never submit original art or anything so valuable you cannot afford to lose it.
☐ Protected — if something gets ruined in the mail, it looks like you didn't care enough to safeguard a package of your best work — work you want to be remembered for.

CHAPTER 5
WHAT DO YOU NEED TO
KNOW ABOUT THE
MAGAZINE MARKET?

TYPES OF MAGAZINES

Q. *How many different types of magazines are there? Do they require different types of artwork?*

A. For many illustrators, there are only two types of magazines: those that take your work and those that don't. The point here is that the magazine market is wide open and diverse, but there are some basic categories.

Look for magazines in the following categories (the categories are real, the following titles are all fictional): local and regional publications (for example: *Ohio Every Second*, *Dayton's Today!*); trade journals (*Velcro World*, *Industrial Strength*); general audience or consumer periodicals (*American Laugh-styles*); special interest magazines (*Modern Hamster*, *Contemporary Antiques*, *Good Sports*); and in-house or company organs (*Inside This Company*).

Every publication is directed to a particular reader, therefore different magazines require different kinds of artwork. You won't find bizarre illustration in *The Saturday Evening Post*; it wouldn't mesh with the conservative audience.

Every magazine has its own editorial tone and visual tenor. The editor and art director make sure the graphics and text work together, and that the flavor of the magazine is consistent throughout.

When a certain story lends itself to a particular treatment, the art director goes to the artist who best fits the bill. Some publications (children's magazines, for instance) take a wider range of work. At every magazine, the art director tries to match an artist's approach with the story and style dictated.

WHAT MAGAZINES NEED

Q. *What freelance skills are needed by magazines?*

A. Copy and illustration share the pages of all periodicals. Magazines want illustrators, photographers, stylists (hair, food, fashion), model makers, prop builders, designers, production artists, calligraphers, copywriters, and editors.

Magazines look for artists who can do four-color or black-and-white illustration. Because many magazines can't afford four-color reproduction throughout the publication, they may require you to supply amberlith flips or shaded vellum overlays for multi-color (two- or three-color) work. Artists who can do this mechanical pre-separation are in demand.

Many magazines, such as special interest publications, lean toward a conceptual approach. Other publications, such as regional and trade magazines, are journalistic in nature. While some conceptual work may be used, they mostly solicit photorealism to record events as they happen.

All magazines require skilled artists. If your skills are weak, the magazine doesn't need you. Some artists have a very minimal delivery, but, in this case, it is a stylistic manner. Magazines, like any client needing a freelancer, will want professionals with good rendering skills, plus a fine color and design sense.

RESEARCHING THE MARKET

Q. *How do you find out if a magazine accepts freelance artwork?*

A. Call the people you'll be working with—the editor, art director, or art staff—and simply ask. Glance through a sample issue, check the credits within the magazine, and see if the work is done by staffers or contributors. Check the masthead; all magazines list those vital folks who create the periodical.

Use the creative directories. Most artists include a client roster in their advertising. While you'll have to research contacts and addresses, you'll cull a long catalog of potential customers from these lists. Also consult reference annuals such as *Artist's Market* for magazines that seek freelance illustration.

FINDING THE LOOK

Q. *How do you analyze the "tone" of a magazine so you'll send appropriate samples?*

FUNNY BUSINESS

With over 10,000 drawings published to date, Sherburne, New York illustrator Randy Glasbergen has a multi-faceted freelance career. He creates "The Better Half" comic strip panel for King Features Syndicate. His cartoons are in *Good House-keeping*, *Cosmopolitan*, *Saturday Evening Post*, and many other publications in twenty-five countries. He does humorous illustration for advertising, calendars, greeting cards, books, magazines, newspapers, posters, and even on dog raincoats!

At age fifteen, Glasbergen sold his first gag cartoon for $5 to what he describes as "a small, 'naughty' book—not a porno publication by any means, but geared towards the adult male. Most of the jokes were pretty simple and dumb, but they used about 450 cartoons per month in three different magazines."

A few months later, he began selling to more mainstream publications. By high school graduation, he was already a fairly well-established magazine cartoonist with sales to the *Saturday Review*, *Changing Times*, *New Woman*, and more.

Glasbergen continued to freelance his magazine cartoons during one year of college as a journalism major. "I didn't study art for fear of losing my individuality as a cartoonist. I was banking a nice monthly income while most of my dorm was writing home for beer money." He decided to drop out and chase his freelance dreams full-time at age nineteen.

"My career has snowballed, but this snowball has rolled uphill! Basically, as my work improved, sales increased, and one opportunity led to another." Glasbergen's first syndicated panel ("Howie") lasted two years and was not a great success. But syn-dicate executives, now familiar with his work, subsequently invited him to take over the writing and drawing of "The Better Half." Glasbergen relates that his experience as a cartoonist also involved him in humorous illustration. A magazine editor acquainted with Glasbergen's cartoons invited him to illustrate an article, and later, a children's book.

"I dabbled in humorous illustration from the start, but only became seriously and aggressively involved in 1983. Prior to this, the quality of my drawings was not adequate for this sort of work. At that time I began to send flyers and cards, really soliciting assignments. I began experimenting with the *Black Book*, *American Showcase*, and *R.S.V.P.* directories, but I never tried personal visits. I prefer to let my work speak for itself. No one single promotional tool has been perfect for me. They all work to one degree or another. Plain old fate plays a big role—having your work seen by the right person at the right time for the right job. Overall, I don't think it matters how you get your work seen, just as long as it gets seen."

Glasbergen's favorite and most successful form of self-promotion is his complete portfolio mailers. Sent to one hundred to three hundred clients (and potential clients) every month, each mailer contains:

- A personalized cover letter.
- An alphabetized list of previous clients.
- Ten to twenty quality photocopies of recent work, briefly described and fully labeled.
- A color sample.
- A reply card.

All these materials are inserted in a pocket folder marked "Portfolio," and completely labeled with Glasbergen's name, address, and phone number.

"It costs me about $300 to $400 each month, and the task would be impossible without my word processor, database, and copying machine. Sending out full-sized portfolios may seem inefficient, but I've had great results. This approach has been extremely effective. I get an enthusiastic response and enough work to keep me busy and happy. I like making the 'bigger effort.' It's like dating: Do you try to win a girl's heart by tossing her a piece of candy

LITTLE EGG UPON THE GROUND, USED TO BE SO SAFE AND ROUND...

Glasbergen's illustration work for Phi Delta Kappan (shown here) came after about twelve years of periodic cartoon sales. The magazine initially sent Glasbergen sporadic assignments. This eventually led to what he calls "a ton of work," including this "animated drawing that really tells a story." The piece is in his portfolio and is included as part of his mailed samples.

or by sending her an attractively wrapped box filled with candy? I prefer to send the latter, disguised as a portfolio.

"It's also very important to mention the value of a good fax machine these days. My fax is just as important as a pencil! Sending roughs or receiving layouts in as little as thirty seconds, I can deliver my sketches faster than if I were working in the same building. If you're going to establish a freelance career, I think a fax must be considered as essential as your phone, your paints, and your eyes."

In his own career, Glasbergen feels that being diversified is very important. "I'm not totally dependent on one single type of work for my entire income. The syndicate work, my ongoing magazine cartoon sales, plus humorous illustration assignments support each other. When one source of income is a little slow, another source picks up the slack. With three horses sharing the load, no one single horse is under too great a strain—and the cowboy sleeps a lot better at night because of it.

"So, if you're really good at greeting cards, don't limit yourself to just that. Learn how to do a second or third specialty. And don't sit around waiting for things to happen. Be active and aggressive and make things happen for you. Take advantage of every opportunity. If a door is opened for you, even just a crack, stick your nose in! You must show people what you can do for them. How can you fill their needs? Being honest, they don't care about your needs—but you must care about theirs! Freelancing is a business—part of the time you must be a salesperson, not just an artist.

"The best part of freelancing is that every day has the potential of being Christmas. Will Santa bring me a shiny new assignment today? Will one of Santa's helpers call me on the phone today with a special surprise? What will I find when I unwrap the goodies in the mailbox today?" Glasbergen is careful to add that Santa doesn't come every day. "But each day has the *potential*, and that's usually enough to keep me excited until the next visit!"

A. A magazine must establish a consistent, distinctive look. Its style—the "tone" of the magazine—should be evident as soon as you glance at the cover.

Send for a sample or go to the library and look at all the recent issues available. Study the illustrations a magazine uses; look at editorial content, think about the subject matter. Is the magazine conservative or progressive? Hip or traditional? Is it politically left or right? Does it specialize in hard-hitting exposés or does it feature stories on food, travel, or fashion? Are the visuals appropriate? Are art and photography conceptual or realistic?

Compare any two magazines (*Life* to *Rolling Stone*, for example), and you should instantly get an impression of what these periodicals are all about. If you don't, the magazine is in trouble because it's not directly addressing its target audience.

EDITOR OR ART DIRECTOR?

Q. *Do you send samples to the editor or to the art director? Do most magazines have an art director?*

A. Send your submission to the art director. Most magazines have an art director (plus, if they're big enough, maybe an associate art director or possibly an assistant art director). Some do not. In these cases the editor or publisher—often one and the same person—reviews art submissions.

Do your homework and establish the appropriate contact at the magazine. Don't forward a portfolio unless you have a specific name or know which department accepts submissions.

Steve Miller, the art director at *Children's Playmate* magazine, gives an important piece of advice. "Never send a portfolio unless you've got return postage guaranteed. If you want your material returned, pay for it. If you don't want the stuff back, fine. Leave it up to the art director. She or he can either put it in the 'tickler' file or drop it in a round file (the waste can)."

One phone call should do the trick; but if you cannot come up with a name (perhaps the position or its occupant is in transition), label your promo, "ATTENTION: ART DIRECTOR" (or "ART DEPARTMENT" or "ART BUYER"). At the outset, this is okay, but when you want to establish or maintain personal correspondence with the magazine, make it a point to get the name of the art buyer as soon as possible.

BEST MAGAZINES FOR BEGINNERS

Q. *Which type of magazine would be good to start with?*

A. Think about the magazines you enjoy most. Browse the library and the newsstand. Look at all you can, then dream a little—visualize where you'd like to be, with whom you'd love to work.

Some feel there is no "best" place for the beginner to start; that all the markets are good—if you're good, why not start right at the top? But trying to start your freelance career at *Time* will probably be like kissing the business end of a shark—good luck!

Others recommend a conservative gambit. Start with local newspapers, work your way up to lesser-known magazines, and eventually move on to larger or more prestigious publications. Begin with small staffs, operations where you won't get lost or mired in the red tape of the big companies. Work at the modest periodicals, accept the low fees to get published credits, and gradually climb the ladder to the heady atmosphere of the big time.

CULTIVATING A VARIETY

Q. *Is it better to have a specific magazine in mind to submit work to, or to send samples to a variety of magazines?*

A. Don't limit your submissions to one type of magazine, or worse yet, one magazine only. Submit to as many magazines as you have a mind to, as many as you can. Freelancing is a numbers game—your livelihood depends on the total drawings you sell. In all likelihood, one client or one type of client won't support or sustain your business. Your style must meet the needs of a variety of magazines if you're to succeed in the magazine market.

There's no reason to wait for the return of a submission or a reaction to your material. Regardless of how prompt the response, remember that there's too much lag time between your submission and a buyer's reply to warrant exclusivity.

SIMULTANEOUS SUBMISSIONS

Q. *Can you send the same illustrations to several magazines at the same time?*

A. Yes, absolutely. Your initial advertising should be somewhat general in scope. You'd have to be prolific—not to mention incredibly rich—to send a different promo to every vendor on your list! Follow ups and portfolios should be targeted to specific clients, but the same illustrations can be sent to several magazines at the same time.

Be aware of audience overlap, however. While wonderfully silly, is that funny drawing of Mother Goose something the art director of *Field and Stream* really wants? Make sure any illustration sent to a variety of magazines will meet the needs of all those buyers.

POSTAL PREFERENCE

Q. *Why are magazines more open to submissions through the mail?*

A. Because art directors are busy people, receiving samples through the mail is an efficient use of their time. But what about the artist's time, energy, and finances? Magazines probably see more people through the mail simply because it's much cheaper and easier to send samples than to visit the office.

Say the periodical is in Cincinnati, and you're in Indianapolis. You've got to drop everything and drive two and a half hours to get there and two and a half hours home. You have no guarantee that you're going to get a job out of all this. When you weigh the costs and risks of doing business through the mail, there is no comparison.

COMMISSIONED VS. UNSOLICITED PIECES

Q. *Do magazines generally buy mailed submissions or do they commission most pieces?*

A. Advertise with completed samples, but don't try to *sell* a finished, unsolicited illustration. Consumer and special interest publications invariably commission artwork for spe-

cific assignments. However, literary magazines often buy existing art because they allow artwork to stand on its own.

DIRECTORIES

Q. *Where do I find listings of magazines?*

A. Listings of magazines can be found at most libraries. Consult the following: *Artist's Market*, *Writer's Market*, *Magazine Industry Marketplace*, the *Standard Periodical Directory*, the *Gebbie Press-All-in-One-Directory*, the *Gale Directory of Publications* (formerly *Ayer's*), and *Ulrich's International Periodicals Directory*.

NEWSSTAND RESEARCH

Q. *Many newsstands carry current magazines. Can you arrange to look at them to get addresses?*

A. I often jot down information about a new publication at the newsstand, but I have always cleared it with the clerk or owner beforehand. Introduce yourself, state your purpose, and express your thanks.

INDUSTRY MAGAZINES

Q. *Are there magazines that cover the magazine industry?*

A. Try *Folio*, *Confetti*, or *Magazine Design & Production*. Look also at *Upper & Lower Case*, *Print* (and their annual Regional Design issue, too), *Step by Step Graphics*, *HOW*, *Graphis*, *Advertising Age*, *Ad Week*, *Art Product News*, *Art Direction*, and *Communication Arts*.

ORGANIZATIONS

Q. *Are there organizations you can join to get to know more magazine illustrators or designers?*

A. Professional organizations you might join are: The Graphic Artists Guild, Society of Publication Designers, American Institute of Graphic Arts (AIGA), or the Society of Illustrators. Consult the City and Regional Magazine Association (CRMA), the Society of Photographers and Artist Representatives (SPAR), Society of Typographic Arts (STA), and your local art directors club.

DEVELOP A POINT
OF VIEW

"I was fortunate to have my first piece published while still a student," New York City illustrator Joe Ciardiello says. "I was in the latter half of my second year (of a three-year program) at Parsons' illustration department. They had a deal with the rock music magazine *Crawdaddy* (now defunct). Since their offices were right down the street from the school, the art director would come by the class and hand out an assignment based on an article that would be in the magazine. He would return about a week later and critique the assignment. The best piece would run in the magazine."

While Ciardiello's work was not picked, he did get back to *Crawdaddy* with his portfolio and was eventually called in for an assignment. "It was a little spot, paying $35, and I was thrilled—I had that all-important tearsheet before I actually got out. This helped a lot. I also had a couple of color pieces printed in the yearbook, and in Parsons' promotional book. This gave me a foot in the door, made it a little

easier. It looked like someone had already taken the risk and tried a new person."

Graduating in the spring of 1974, Ciardiello began freelancing in September of that year. His first freelance assignments involved textbook illustration and magazine work. "The trade magazines tend to pay a little less than regular consumer magazines, but they commission a lot of artwork, particularly with spots. It's a good source for newcomers to obtain printed pieces."

Ciardiello's start was a bit rocky. With a sigh, he remembers a certain spread from *Playboy* magazine. He had graduated from Parsons only two years earlier, and this was to be his biggest paying job to date. Unfortunately, the assignment was rejected, but Ciardiello was never informed. "I only found out months later when I was sent the rejection—a kill fee. I was devastated. Any inflated ego I had been developing during those early years was quickly gone."

He counsels other freelancers to be prepared for rejection when starting out. "It could be a job that just doesn't go for whatever reason, being rejected from annuals, or from annual shows to which you submit work. But you must be able to separate it emotionally, to say, 'This is not a reflection of me personally. It just wasn't appropriate for whatever reason.' This is hard to do, especially in the beginning. You've got to keep a perspective on it."

Ciardiello says to present your portfolio in a professional manner when approaching magazine markets. "Avoid work that looks too obviously like a class project. Avoid work that looks experimental for the sake of being experimental. Stick to good work geared to the type of client to whom you're showing your book. It's always better to have fewer pieces if they're really good than a ton of boring pages. Even if it's only a handful of great material, it's better than a giant mediocre portfolio."

He also suggests showing one style. "It will confuse art directors if they see a different style on every page in your book. Everybody is pretty much a specialist, so why go to someone who does a variety of styles? Art directors have such a choice of people—they want to peg you and get a sense of what your work is all about. If you do a little of everything, there's no reason for them to go with you. It's better if they see one direction."

When Ciardiello was starting out, he found most of his assignments through making cold calls. "Maybe out of ten or fifteen phone calls I landed two or three appointments, and I'd fill up my weeks with as many appointments as I could get. Most of my jobs came from those phone calls and going on portfolio interviews. It was a difficult but positive experience, because I was very excited about my future as an illustrator. The excitement overpowered everything else. That motivated me to keep trying. I didn't go a long time without work; it wasn't steady, but people were starting to use me.

"Be conscious of your self-promotion all the time," Ciardiello advises. You can't afford to just sit back and say, 'Well, I'm busy now and it's going to continue this way, and I don't have to do too much about it.' I think you always have to be aware of how many people are out there doing the same thing. Always have a mailer, even if it's an inexpensive one at first—something to either leave behind or put in the mail to potential clients." He adds that art directors won't know by looking at your mailer if you've only been out of school a year. "If they like what they see, you can get a job."

Hailing from Staten Island, Ciardiello stayed on his home turf when he began freelancing. "There's so much work in New York City that I pretty much focused on that area. Fortunately, I was able to live at home for a couple of years after graduation. What little money I made in the beginning I was able to reinvest in terms of self-promotion. I didn't have to worry about meeting bills."

Ciardiello recommends *not* looking for a full-time job (if at all possible) if you are also freelancing. "Taking a full-time job limits you for possible rush assignments or just having the time to go out and see people and get your book together. It's my experience that freelance illustration requires all of your attention. Doing anything else means it's going to take that much longer to get started. If you want to be an illustrator, illustration is what you really have to focus on. Develop a style, a point of view, and a direction you want to pursue, then keep your portfolio consistent in that area."

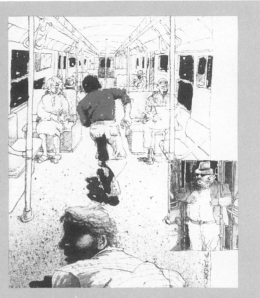

© Joe Ciardiello. Used with permission.

Based on the strength of a mailer, Joe Ciardiello was called on his first job for the Sunday magazine of the *New York Daily News*. Chosen for his "journalistic" approach, the energy of that illustration made Ciardiello the first choice to do "Song of the Subway." The art director for the *News* needed his visuals to tell a story and Ciardiello was handpicked as a direct result of his great work on the previous assignment. The vibrant illustration has won an award from the Society of Publication Designers (appearing in a subsequent annual), and was in Ciardiello's portfolio.

CHAPTER FIVE
CHECKLISTS

Basic magazine categories:
☐ Local and regional publications.
☐ Trade journals.
☐ General audience or consumer periodicals.
☐ Special interest magazines.
☐ In-house or company organs.

To find out if a magazine accepts freelance artwork:
☐ Call the editor, art director, or art staff.
☐ Glance through sample issues, check the credits and masthead.
☐ Use the creative directories and cull a catalog of potential customers from the artists' lists.
☐ Consult reference annuals.

To analyze the "tone" of a magazine:
☐ Send for a sample.
☐ Go the library and look at recent issues.
☐ Compare magazines.

When sending samples:
☐ Send your submissions to the art director.
☐ Most magazines have an art director—if not, send your samples to the editor or publisher (sometimes the editor and publisher are one and the same person).

☐ Always send a portfolio with return postage guaranteed.
☐ If you cannot find a specific name, label your promo "ATTENTION: ART DIRECTOR" (or "ART DEPARTMENT" or "ART BUYER").

Exploring the magazine market:
☐ Browse all magazine outlets.
☐ Begin with local magazines or those with small staffs.
☐ Work your way up to lesser-known magazines and eventually to larger or more prestigious publications.

Sending illustrations to several magazines at once:
☐ Your initial advertising should be generic.
☐ Follow-ups can be targeted to specific clients.
☐ Portfolios should be targeted to specific clients.
☐ Any illustration sent to a variety of magazines should meet the needs of all those buyers.

To find magazine listings consult:
- [ ] *Artist's Market.*
- [ ] *Writer's Market.*
- [ ] *Standard Periodical Directory.*
- [ ] *Gebbie Press All-in-One Directory.*
- [ ] *Gale Directory of Publications* (formerly *Ayer's*).
- [ ] *Ulrich's International Periodicals Directory.*
- [ ] *Magazine Industry Marketplace.*

Magazines that cover the magazine industry:
- [ ] *Folio.*
- [ ] *Print.*
- [ ] *Confetti.*
- [ ] *Magazine Design & Production.*
- [ ] *Art Direction.*
- [ ] *Upper & Lower Case.*
- [ ] *Step by Step Graphics.*
- [ ] *HOW.*
- [ ] *Graphis.*
- [ ] *Advertising Age.*
- [ ] *Ad Week.*
- [ ] *Art Product News.*
- [ ] *Art Direction.*
- [ ] *Communication Arts.*

Organizations to join:
- [ ] Graphic Artists Guild.
- [ ] Society of Publication Designers.
- [ ] American Institute of Graphic Arts (AIGA).
- [ ] Society of Illustrators.
- [ ] City and Regional Magazine Association (CRMA).
- [ ] Society of Photographers and Artist Representatives.
- [ ] Society of Typographic Arts.
- [ ] Your local art directors club.

CHAPTER 6
HOW DO YOU SELL WORK TO NEWSPAPERS?

TYPES OF NEWSPAPERS

Q. *How many different types of newspapers are there? Do they require different types of artwork?*

A. The basic format of a newspaper doesn't vary much since the primary function is to report news. However, there are many types of news publications. You will find neighborhood newsletters, local and regional newspapers, big city newspapers with a national circulation (the *New York Times*), newspapers with a national scope (*U.S.A. Today*), and tabloids (the *National Enquirer*).

Within the pages of any newspaper, different types of artwork are required. A freelance illustrator and staff artist for the *Dayton Daily News*, Ted Pitts says that a beginner wanting to freelance for newspapers can be a specialist. If you want to work for newspapers, Pitts says, "You'll have to have several different approaches that fit different situations because you'll have to illustrate both serious subjects for the editorial and op-ed pages and humorous ones for features."

SKILLS FOR NEWSPAPERS

Q. *What freelance skills are needed by newspapers?*

A. You can freelance as an illustrator, designer, production artist, and calligrapher. Newspapers also look for artists to create informational graphics—maps, charts, and diagrams—as well as the researchers to develop these projects.

Black-and-white illustrations are the bread and butter of newspaper illustration, but thanks to the influence of *USA Today*, color is now exploding in the industry.

FREELANCING VS. STAFF

Q. *Should I freelance with our local paper or would it be better to try for a staff illustrator's position?*

A. The staff illustrator's position is highly coveted, and competition is stiff. A better title for the job probably is "staff artist," with a job description most likely encompassing page design and the creation of informational graphics.

There aren't many staff positions for illustrators at newspapers. Throw in the economics of hiring a full-time staff person as opposed to a freelancer, and your chances are better as an independent.

CALL TO QUERY

Q. *How do you find out if a newspaper accepts freelance artwork?*

A. Newspapers don't use illustration for fast-breaking, hard news stories. Due to the time factor, very few news graphics could be done freelance.

The sections most open to freelance work include the op-ed page. Features or magazine sections that are planned well in advance of publication also are freelance possibilities. Here you are dealing with events, trends and ideas.

To find out if a newspaper accepts freelance work, call the editor, art director, or art staff, and ask. Consult the *Editor & Publisher's Yearbook* (and the weekly magazine *Editor and Publisher*), and *Artist's Market*.

ANALYZING THE "TONE"

Q. *How do you analyze the "tone" of a newspaper so you'll send appropriate samples?*

A. Compare two newspapers (the *Washington Post* and the *New York Daily News*, for instance) to contrast those qualities that make each publication unique and individual.

Determine a newspaper's philosophical content and political position. Analyze and evaluate subject matter while examining writing styles. Then, study all illustration and photography. Is the art conceptual or straightforward? Do visuals and copy mesh to better convey the point of the story? Do you agree with the editorial stance? In your evaluation, does the artwork succeed?

Illustrator Tom Graham says, "I think it is

TIMELY EXPOSURE

Tom Graham was trained as a painter, but came to realize that, "I was not going to be the next Jasper Johns. I saw no point in living in a roach-infested, cold-water flat while developing the next big thing that may or may not fly in the fashion-conscious downtown art scene. It wasn't right for me."

Graham chose to develop his work commercially. "I decided to make art that solved a problem and get paid for it. In retrospect I can see clearly that I was cut out to be an illustrator, not a cutting-edge fine artist. But those 'artist' years were the best in my life, a time when I learned as much about my art as I did myself. It is no great hardship to be young and poor when you can proudly call yourself an artist."

It took Graham several years to make the transition, during which time he practiced carpentry and took night courses at the School of Visual Arts. "These classes helped me tremendously. They exposed me to professional illustrators; they trained me to be a problem-solver, and to develop a critical faculty, to ask myself hard questions about my own work as well as that of others.

"Two years later I had a decent portfolio, but was relatively ignorant about the markets and consequently wasted much time. I had been getting the odd job here and there (textile designs, cartoons, placemats for restaurants, anything to pay the rent) and slowly learning the game. I was still young enough not to mind pounding the pavement, making calls, visiting offices. The rejection rate was high."

Graham, however, knew someone at the *New York Times*. Although they had established a previous relationship, there was no guarantee of a job there. In fact, as Graham tells it, "I was a bit intimidated to visit the *Times'* offices, but I wanted this designer to see my recent work. He took photocopies and promised to keep me in mind. I eventually got a small spot asssignment, and the designer has continued to call me for various jobs. We've developed a good working relationship, brainstorming ideas that usually work.

The *Times* assignments established Graham's freelance career. "Everybody looks at this newspaper, and many people called me with jobs. I'll be forever grateful to this particular designer for seeing something in my work when few others did."

If you're considering working with newspapers, Graham suggests a few points to consider. First is style. "Unless a newspaper uses a good coated stock, subtlety is not to be relied upon. A style with hard tones, strong areas of black, and boldy stated tones will succeed. Line art is best, of course, but a painting would work. It stands to reason that if your style is ethereal, with a layered wash look, you might not be successful."

Another skill required in newspaper work is speed. "The turnaround time for the work I have done has ranged from a few hours to, at most, a few days. It would be a serious impediment to work for a daily and have an elaborate, time-consuming oil painting technique, though I suppose for a Sunday or quarterly supplement it might be acceptable.

"Stylistically I think it pays to develop something a little bit different than what is out there already, keeping in mind you have to be comfortable with it. It has to come out of you. Maybe trends sell, but I suggest being true to your own likes and dislikes. Most art directors are hiring you to give your point of view about a given subject. A lasting career is built when you bring something new to the arena. A career spent knocking off the latest hot style will last only as long as each style does."

Small spot illustrations continue to be Graham's bread and butter. "They give me time and a financial base to develop other aspects of my art, including children's books, other publishing ventures, self-promotion, and painting for the pure joy of painting."

important to objectively analyze the look a newspaper is currently printing. Chances are, they will not stray far afield from that look. If what they are currently printing really turns you on, and you feel you would fit right in, maybe even do it better, then proceed."

EDITOR VS. ART DIRECTOR

Q. *Do you send samples to the editor or the art director? Do most newspapers have an art director?*

A. As a rule of thumb, I'd send to the art director, unless instructed otherwise.

It's okay to submit samples to the editor. The editor or publisher—frequently one and the same person—often reviews art submissions. Some newspapers, especially smaller ones, may not have an art director. Maybe administrative responsibilities are shared or rotated among staff members, or the chief artist acts as art director. Perhaps the features editor is the freelance coordinator. Many papers have an assistant managing editor for graphics or designate an illustration buyer.

Establish the appropriate contact at the newspaper by doing your homework. Don't forward a portfolio unless you have a specific name or know the correct department accepting submissions.

START LOCALLY

Q. *What newspapers would be good to start with?*

A. Start with a community newsletter, then work your way up to the local newspaper and beyond. Begin with small-staffed operations, work at the modest publications. Accept the low fees for published credits and experience and gradually climb the ladder. It also does not hurt to do a few "freebies" to get on track.

SIMULTANEOUS SUBMISSIONS

Q. *Is it better to have a specific newspaper in mind to submit work to, or do I send samples to a variety of newspapers?*

A. Don't submit to one paper at a time—there's no reason to wait for the return of a submis-

sion or a reaction to your material. If there's only one newspaper in town, they may or may not buy freelance, so local options may be limited.

Follow-ups can—and portfolios should—be targeted to specific clients. Even here (if the drawings are appropriate), the same illustrations can be sent to several newspapers at the same time.

COMMISSION OR SUBMISSION?

Q. *Do newspapers generally buy mailed submissions or do they commission most pieces?*

A. Newspapers generally commission artwork for a specific article. News breaks fast, and current events are exactly that—a mailed submission will probably not be timely for a newspaper. If they use freelance work, the art director will certainly want to spend money on art that fits the copy—not "comes close" or "might work with some imagination."

Send finished art, but not the originals, as advertising. Don't hope or expect the editor to bend the news around your samples.

DIRECTORIES OF NEWSPAPERS

Q. *Where do you find listings of newspapers? Are there magazines that cover the newspaper industry?*

A. Listings of newspapers can be found in the *Editor and Publisher Yearbook*. Also consult *Working Press of the Nation*, the *Gale Directory of Publications*, and *Artist's Market*. Read the *Columbia Journalism Review*, *Editor and Publisher*, the *Washington Journalism Review*, and the *Artist's Magazine*.

ORGANIZATIONS

Q. *Are there organizations you can join to get to know more newspaper illustrators?*

A. Your local ad club is a good place to start. Join the Graphic Artist's Guild. Look into the Society of Newspaper Design, National Cartoonists Society, the Association of American Editorial Cartoonists, and the Society of Illustrators.

GETTING INTO PRINT

On his way to a law career, illustrator Ted Pitts got side-tracked. After passing the bar, and while looking for a job in the Dayton, Ohio area, Pitts answered an advertisement for a newspaper artist. "I didn't know there was such a thing as a newspaper artist," he relates. "I was vaguely aware of editorial cartooning, but that was about it."

Pitts had no experience or real qualifications. "I had drawn since I was very small and had kept up with it," he says, "plus I almost majored in art in college, but decided not to." With nothing to lose, Pitts brashed his way into a portfolio review. "Nobody else who was any good applied, and I got the job. I had to promise not to quit and become a lawyer, though."

Ten years later, Pitts is still drawing for the newspaper. With the hindsight of a successful freelance career and as a staff artist for Dayton papers and Florida's *Miami Herald*, Pitts assesses those early days. "What you lack when you first start out is consistency. At some point I learned what most of my work lacked at that time was just concentration. Once I finally started to really concentrate, the quality of my illustration was much better.

"It was really a good thing to get the job at the Dayton paper right off the bat," Pitts comments about his staff position. "I was doing three, four, sometimes five drawings a night, and I had to learn to draw very, very fast. You can see the different levels of expertise develop as you do that."

Pitts has found that working with newspapers differs from working for other markets. "My experience is that newspapers art-direct you less than advertising," says Pitts. "A newspaper generally sends you a story and says, 'Get back with some ideas.' They tend *not* to say, 'We want a drawing of such-and-such,' which is the way it is in advertising. You have to have the ability to come up with your own ideas, more so than in advertising.

"I've had more lead time on some newspaper stories than I've had on magazine or advertising jobs. It just depends on the client. The *Detroit Free Press* called once with an assignment due the next day. They knew my work, and my ability to create relatively quickly. I did the job that night, then ran it out to the airport at 11 P.M."

Pitts says that most staff positions are few and far between. "If you can get a staff illustrator's position on a newspaper, you've got a steady income and you could do a greater volume of work. If you're doing a greater volume of work, obviously your work's going to get better.

"But the people being hired at newspapers right now are being hired to work on the Macintosh and create graphics, as opposed to illustration. Usually everyone is doing everything, which is the way it has to be if your staff artists are all illustrators and talented in that direction."

When he began freelancing, Pitts experienced the same self-doubt that many other freelancers experience. "You know whether or not you're good enough to crack into the national markets, and that's what I wanted to do. I wanted to do editorial illustrations for magazines because they use better paper and have a wider circulation. But I didn't think I was good enough when I first started out."

When he eventually felt ready, with five years of credits and credentials, Pitts created a far different book than the one that landed him his staff position. "It's funny how you decide to whom you send your samples," he muses. "There's the art director who sometimes is a very famous person, who everybody knows and probably gets more mail than he can read. Then there are all these associate art directors, and you tend to pick out the one with the nicest name, or send it to all of them, which is what I've started to do recently. I send it to all of them because it's been my experience that you might get a little job from an associate art director, which might get you another job with the art director. You can get your foot in the door with an associate art director who likes your stuff."

Pitts prefers to mail his portfolio rather than personally showing it. "I put together three 9"x12" portfolios, which cost about $300, containing about twenty pieces of work. I make 5"x7" prints – 8"x10" prints of pieces that I like. So I have three separate, but identical portfolios coming and going to people at the same time.

"I call first, as I've got a substantial investment in the portfolio, and I do want the art directors to look at it. Most of the time I find these people extremely nice and very conscientious. They're not casual about it, and they want to have time to see your work. So they'll say, 'Send it on this date.' I enclose an SASE, and mail it all in another envelope. This costs about $7 or $8.

"My self-promotion is getting to be more and more regular," Pitts says. "My current strategy is to send three or four or more pieces per year, spaced over a month or two-month period – just keep reminding these people that you exist.

"I have a list of over a hundred people to whom I send editorial mailings," he tells us. "You've got to spend some money, reinvest your capital in your business, and do more mailers.

"I think it's imperative that you keep sending to people so they will eventually know your work. There's a certain amount of luck in freelancing, but a lot of it is perseverence and self-promotion. It's one day finally saying that the illustration I'm seeing in a particular magazine is just not as good as my stuff, and I'm going to pester that art director until he gives me one of those jobs. I'm going to show him or her that I should've been used all along!

"You *have* to promote yourself. People must see your work. If you don't have an agent, the only way for that to happen is for you to do it yourself." Pitts has an agent, who secures his advertising jobs, while Pitts sells his own work to editorial markets.

"Initially, I tried to keep my promotion as cheap as possible, and directed it toward a specific group of people in editorial. The first mailer I ever did as a freelancer cost me $32; I've figured out that I received about $20,000 to $25,000 worth of work out of it over a period of years. People tend to keep these things in their file and go back and look at them. You may see the fruit of what you're doing now a year later. While this isn't going to pay your bills next

© Ted Pitts. Used with permission.

An active freelancer, Pitts is also a staff artist for the *Dayton Daily News*. "Football Players" was done for the newspaper to illustrate a story on a national championship bowl game. Used as a portfolio piece, it also circulates in Pitts' sample packages and markets his distinctive approach.

month, it might take that long.

"Conversely, I was in the *American Illustration Showcase* once and didn't get very much work out of it. The reality of that is it is expensive, but I'll do it again. You can make it back in one freelance advertising job, but you have to get that job. These things generally take a couple of years, unless you're a bright star that everyone wants to latch on to.

"Enter contests to get published in annuals. I've probably gotten as much work out of this as anything. I still get calls from my piece in *American Illustration*, and I've used print overruns of this page as a promotion tool, as well.

"Follow up mailings by talking to people in person. If you put a voice with what you're sending out, you're going to get more work."

As an end note, Pitts says, "On my recent mailers, I've decided to send art that I really like. If it doesn't sell, fine – I'm still going to do work I like. I haven't gotten a call yet. But that's all right – I will someday, from some very intelligent art director!"

ART THAT SPEAKS FOR ITSELF

When David Catrow graduated high school in 1971 he didn't quite know what he wanted to do. "If I were to take the cue from other people in my class," he says, "most of my classmates wanted to graduate and overthrow the government." Catrow himself joined the Navy, then went to Kent State University, where he majored in biology.

Since Catrow illustrated most of his classnotes, some instructors suggested that he go into medical illustration. "I worked for a teaching hospital with many doctors getting papers published, and with the education department. I'd charge $20 an hour to do slides for them. It worked out fine."

However, Catrow didn't get as much satisfaction out of it as he would have liked. "Maybe I'm sort of an idealist," he remarks. "I thought there was more to life, to your job—that you were supposed to be happy for eight, ten hours a day, five days a week.

Artistically, I wanted to branch out and get some variety, so during that time I was doing freelance work for the *Akron Beacon Journal* and the *Cleveland Plain Dealer*." He illustrated for the Sunday magazine and daily features. "If their staff illustrators were booked up, they'd sometimes come to me."

He began to draw humorous illustrations, mostly unpublished political cartoons. "I did these things on my own, and called Ray Osrin, the political cartoonist with the *Cleveland Plain Dealer*, who in turn referred me to Mike Peters of the *Dayton Daily News*. Mike remembered me when his publisher moved over to another paper in Springfield, Ohio. The publisher called me up and asked if I wanted to come in for an interview. I came down, and that's how I got to be staff illustrator for the *Springfield News-Sun*.

"My first portfolio contained some illustrations on colocystectomy," Catrow tells us, "and I had some funny chalk drawings that I'd created: creatures with one foot and horns out of the forehead and things like that—light, children's bookish sort of things. It showed some drawing style, and I thought that was the most important thing.

"The portfolio case I had was something I'd gotten when I was in high school, one of those tie jobs. It was a black thing about 2'x3' and it had a little flap that you'd tuck in to keep your artwork from spilling all over the sidewalk. You'd have shoestrings that you'd tie on the three remaining sides that weren't hinged.

"It was completely destroyed. It was just all frayed and torn—I had used it as backing when cutting with my X-Acto knife. I realized that I had to do something about this portfolio."

Catrow decided to build his own case the night before a portfolio review. "It looked like a coffin for a flounder or something like that—big and bulky. I put all my junk in there—my pictures of gallbladders and brains and livers—and took it in," Catrow chuckles. "Some art directors would just look at it and laugh. I'm sure as soon as I left they said, 'What a dork! He comes in here with a wooden box, showing us gallbladders—*but he can draw!*' At least I hope that's what they said. Indeed, I got work from that portfolio. My very first experience illustrating a story was a direct

Before laying their beloved Ayatollah to rest, millions of mourners treat the Imam to some traditional Iranian beach volleyball.

A busy freelancer, David Catrow also works full-time at the *Springfield News-Sun.* The paper's editorial cartoonist and staff illustrator, Catrow is syndicated nationally by Copley News Service. Catrow's editorial work, like this 1989 cartoon, initially appears in the *News-Sun* (who own first publication rights). He does three cartoons a week for his home paper, and these—unless the gags are of purely local, state, or regional interest—are automatically used by the syndicate. Catrow estimates that about ninety percent of his cartoons deal with national issues.

result—the *Beacon Journal* gave me a cover and some inside illustrations for their Sunday magazine."

Catrow makes the point that you should always show work you like. "Put in ten things that you're really excited about—and it doesn't have to be just what the art directors are looking for. Obviously, you wouldn't try to get a job as an aircraft designer with a bunch of organs in a portfolio. But you want to display stuff that you enjoyed doing. Hopefully, when the art director looks at your book, she'll say, 'This guy has talent and he enjoys his work. He's probably serious about it.'

"Art directors, due to the nature of their projects, can't spend a whole lot of time or money finding someone who specializes in, let's say, heat pumps. Many times it will be a new artist they'll see. If that person can draw an elephant, or a house, or a car, he or she could probably draw a heat pump too, and art directors realize that."

As his style has evolved, so has Catrow's self-confidence. "I think I've gotten more comfortable with what I do," he says. "It's almost like a comic strip artist who is accustomed to the characters he draws. He starts knowing them, and once you become familiar with something, you're able to describe it a whole lot more succinctly.

"Once you get used to your cast of characters, you can weed out all the superfluous stuff. I know my style. I know what works and what doesn't work because I've tried it. A lot of my work now comes across more simply and uncluttered—it looks spontaneous. Before, it looked too labored; I took too much time trying to explain a situation.

"I'm starting to draw *for me*. I think people see that, and know I'm enjoying it. It looks like you waved the magic wand and your feelings that day came out on the paper. When you draw for yourself, this comes across as something very nice, indeed."

The poise expressed in his work gives Catrow an added edge in dealing with art directors. "If you're confident enough about what you do, you can change people's minds. You have to let your art speak for itself."

Does this apply to the beginner as well? According to Catrow, "If you're just starting out and doing everything—heat pumps and dogs—you have to accept art direction and just work with it. Even though you're drawing exactly what they say to draw, you can still be honest and make it your own.

"Sometimes you're just walking a real tight line. You can't deviate too much from what the art directors want, but you still want to make it yours, too. I don't turn down too many jobs because somebody asks me to work in such a controlled situation. While I've refused assignments of this nature, I don't turn them down too often. I can still be creative with that. I can still let myself come through and have fun with it."

The perks of creative independence are always accompanied by the pitfalls of critique and rejection. Catrow cautions, "First realize that people are going to say things that you don't like. While you have to put yourself into your illustration and make it your own thing, if you don't shield yourself some way, it shows up in and affects your work.

"At first my art was just so personal to me that, if art directors said something about a color I had used or a line that I'd made— if they made any mention at all, even an indifferent remark—it would really hurt my feelings. It would take some time to recuperate from that.

"You have to develop a pretty thick skin to go out there and deal with people," Catrow advises. "If you enjoy what you're doing and you're drawing for yourself, then it really doesn't matter what other people think."

Catrow has juggled both a freelance career and a full-time staff job and finds that "it's difficult. I've been drawing all day and the last thing I want to do when I get home is draw again, but I go into the studio and draw again. If I didn't enjoy my job, I'd probably be hanging from some rafter some place with a note pinned to my shirt.

"I do three political cartoons a week and I'm syndicated to about eight hundred newspapers around the country. The *News-Sun* also assigns me quite a bit of illustration—occasionally I feel overwhelmed. But I take the philosophy that you have to draw every day. And you have to put that pressure on yourself to draw on demand because a client isn't going to come up to you and say, 'Here, I want you to draw this when the urge really strikes you.' They're going to say, 'We'd like this done by tomorrow and we'd like to see your roughs in an hour.' They're the client and they're paying you. You have to be disciplined, and a lot of artists aren't. I'm one of the biggest procrastinators in the world. But there are a lot of people who are doing this who are very successful and have never worked for a company or had a health plan in their life. There are freelancers who are very secure doing this.

"It's hard work," Catrow reiterates, "but when you go out and do something every day that you enjoy doing—and I do—it's not called hustling. It's called a vocation. It's even a calling—something religious. I don't think of myself as a hustler, but if I were selling machine equipment, people would say I'm a workaholic."

CHAPTER SIX
CHECKLISTS

There are different types of newspapers:
- ☐ Neighborhood newsletters.
- ☐ Local and regional newspapers.
- ☐ Big city newspapers with a national circulation.
- ☐ Newspapers with a national scope.
- ☐ Tabloids.
- ☐ General interest newspapers.
- ☐ Special interest newspapers.

Directories and magazines covering newspapers:
- ☐ *Editor & Publisher*, the weekly magazine and the *Yearbook*.
- ☐ *Artist's Market*.
- ☐ *Working Press of the Nation*.
- ☐ *Gale Directory of Publications*.
- ☐ *Columbia Journalism Review*.
- ☐ *Washington Journalism Review*.
- ☐ *The Artist's Magazine*.

Organizations affiliated with newspapers:
- ☐ Graphic Artists Guild.
- ☐ Society of Newspaper Design.
- ☐ National Cartoonists Society.
- ☐ Association of American Editorial Cartoonists.
- ☐ Society of Illustrators.

CHAPTER 7

HOW DO YOU SELL WORK TO ADVERTISING AGENCIES?

WHAT AGENCIES DO

Q. *What does an advertising agency do?*

A. That depends upon the agency, because no two agencies are alike. In general, advertising agencies solve marketing problems by communicating what the client wants (and needs) his market to know. To do this, ad agencies develop printed matter, audio, and audiovisual work from concept to finished product.

They create copy and appropriate graphics for ads in magazines and newspapers, produce radio and television commercials, and conceive billboards and direct mail campaigns. Most produce product literature, sales brochures, and other such collateral material. You'll find the larger agencies doing market research and public relations, as well.

ADVERTISING AGENCIES VS. PUBLIC RELATIONS FIRMS

Q. *What's the difference between an ad agency and a public relations firm? How do their freelance needs differ?*

A. Public relations firms assist clients by increasing awareness of their clients' existence, presenting a new image, or even polishing a tarnished reputation.

PR firms attempt to keep you in the limelight with published stories, newspaper articles, television spots and interviews, lectures, book signings or autograph sessions. They'll even create media events and publicity stunts. The high profile created by a PR firm helps position a client favorably in their particular market, works to counteract negative publicity, or establishes a new direction for that client.

Public relations firms produce "indirect advertising," and assignments from PR firms parallel those of ad agencies. Since the full-time staff usually concentrates on marketing research and consulting with clients, PR firms often use freelance artists, writers, and graphic designers. Public relations firms are good places to get work because they generally don't have art departments and are directly aligned with an ad agency or a studio.

SKILLS NEEDED

Q. *What skills do advertising agencies call upon from freelancers?*

A. Agencies use freelancers for keyline and mechanicals, model building, plus illustration of all types in all media. If an agency doesn't have someone in-house with these abilities, a freelancer gets the nod. Small agencies might regularly require a great deal of freelance help. Big agencies may use freelancers only when staff are on leave, or when they have an overflow of work.

Design and production needs are often fulfilled by good freelancers, but you might find that the "fun stuff" stays in-house while the tedious "grunt work" goes to the independent contractors. And, with the dawn of computers and desktop publishing, production and design take far less time and now require computer literacy.

Illustrators are probably the most frequently used freelancers. Even the larger agencies might employ only one or two skilled illustrators. As these folks usually double as art directors or designers, they can't devote the time to daily illustration needs. That's where you, that talented masked artist with the silver portfolio, ride in.

FULL-SERVICE AGENCY

Q. *What is a full-service agency? What is a multimedia agency?*

A. A full-service agency *is* a multimedia agency, working in both broadcast and print. As the term implies, they do it all—from newspaper ads to TV campaigns and audiovisuals, sales literature to direct mail, public relations to market research. A majority of agencies make this claim, but few perform equally well in all areas.

WHEN FREELANCERS ARE NEEDED

Q. *When do agencies use freelance help?*

A. In a large city, many agencies rely on good freelance help. In a regular-sized town, not only are independent contractors called when a special look is needed, but when the regular staff is on vacation, sick leave, maternity leave, or if the agency gets a temporary overflow of work.

For instance, around the Christmas holidays, an agency with many retail clients may be inundated with work. Freelancers may be called in to help through this busy season. As soon as the holidays pass, work levels revert to normal and freelancers are no longer needed.

FINDING SUITABLE AGENCIES

Q. *How do you find agencies that best suit your talents?*

A. Knowing what a particular agency does and who its clients are takes some digging. First, network. Phone the chamber of commerce and the Better Business Bureau for information about local agencies. Talk to your colleagues, check with printers, touch base with businesses that advertise. Ask around and get as much background information about the local advertising scene as you can. The next step is to call the agencies yourself.

You don't even have to ask for the art director, initially. Talk to the receptionist; if he or she doesn't have the answers you need, you'll be directed to someone who does. Simply ask, "What are your specialties? Can or do you use freelancers? In what capacity?"

Remember the three virtues in selling your art: Be persistent, be polite, be positive. If your communication skills are professional, you shouldn't have any problems. You'll find people in this field to be friendly and helpful.

Schedule a portfolio review. While you're there, ask to see the agency's book. It's a legitimate request; I don't think the art director will balk at showing the piece that snagged all those awards last year.

Introduce yourself around town and see what the different agencies are doing, then make up your own mind. Some decisions are made for you. If you work in pen and ink, the Jones Agency, which produces television commercials, probably won't require your services. Of course, Smith Studios next door

might. Smith specializes in printed material and needs an artist of your talents.

But remember, someone at the agency— usually the creative director or art director— will determine whether or not your talents suit *their* needs. Make sure they're aware of your talents.

SPECIALIZATION?

Q. *Should illustrators specialize in a certain product area?*

A. Use common sense. You know best where your strengths lie. Stay busy, but enjoy what you're doing.

Some agencies find a comfortable niche and stay there, believing that specialized experience allows them to create better work. This can be true, but there is a danger of falling into a rut. This also holds true for the freelancer, so don't limit yourself. More flexibility means a wide variety of assignments. More assignments mean better money. Keep all available doors open; only specialize if you freelance in a big city that has more than enough work to support your specialty. Flexibility and variety will allow you to gather pollen from a wider range of flowers.

KNOWING THE MARKET

Q. *How can you tell if ad agencies work with freelancers? How do you know when they need one?*

A. Ask them. Show your book, then market and promote yourself like crazy. It might depend on the size of the agency (a large agency doesn't use as many freelancers as a small one).

Again, if you have referrals, get some background information. If you don't, you'll only find out by making some inquiries yourself.

Obviously, you won't know when they need a freelancer until *they* do. Ms. Theo Stephan, owner and Creative Director at the Real Art Design Group in Dayton, Ohio, says, "A common rule of thumb is, don't call them, they'll call you! Once you've shown your portfolio to the agency, they have a good idea of your capabilities. Drop the art director a short note of thanks after that first meeting. Share your interest in producing work for the agency. Don't grovel or give them starving artist war stories. Act successful, even if you did have to walk twelve miles to the bus stop in a driving Sahara dust storm. Everybody likes working with a winner, not someone who is unsure of themselves!"

WHOM TO CONTACT

Q. *Whom do you contact at an advertising agency?*

A. There's at least one art director at an agency. Big agencies often have a number of art directors. The art director may answer to the creative director.

Whom to talk to? One phone call, and you'll know for sure. Ask the receptionist who the art buyer may be.

Michael Woolley is vice president and creative director at Weber, Geiger, and Kalat, in Dayton, Ohio. Woolley recommends, "The more people who know you and your abilities, the better. The first person to try is the creative director, but also contact art directors, artists, copy chiefs, and copywriters."

PLAYING THE FIELD

Q. *Is it best to work for as many agencies as possible or to get as much work as you can from one or two agencies?*

A. You must get it where you can, depending on the size of your town and the temperament of the advertising community. It would not be wise to do an assignment for one agency, then go directly to the competition and create work of the exact same stripe. Don't expect the first agency to welcome you with open arms afterwards.

There is some paranoia between agencies. Agency A may wonder if you shared marketing strategies or divulged any dark secrets to Agency B. Ask yourself if there is a conflict of interest between two rival accounts. You may never have to deal with this situation, but be aware that it does exist.

WAYS TO BREAK IN

Q. *What is the best way to break into this market?*

A. Agencies use a lot of layout comps (comprehensive sketches of an ad or concept) during client presentations or when pitching an idea to prospective buyers. If you're skilled with markers and can do a good comp, this would be an apt way to break into the market. Use your layout skills to pave the way for future illustration assignments.

If you can, get referrals from people you know in the field who might have agency contacts. Ask them if you can drop their names while making your sales calls: "Hello, my name is so-and-so and I received your name from so-and-so as a possible contact. I'd like to set up an appointment to show my portfolio." Be sure to make your appointment at the agency's convenience.

If you're new in town, join organizations that are frequented by local art directors and creative individuals. There's an ad club in just about every town. Consult the chamber of commerce regarding the names of associations, meeting places, and times.

Put your self-promotion and marketing plan into action. Establish contacts, then don't let them forget you. Send a thank-you note after your initial appointment and follow up with frequent reminders. Call occasionally—stay in touch!

APPROPRIATE SAMPLES

Q. *If you've been doing greeting cards and want to do some advertising work, what samples do you send to an advertising agency?*

A. Don't mix apples and oranges. Ad agency art directors won't be interested in your card samples as greeting cards, per se. You won't be writing copy, so your cutesy puns are only good for a snicker as they turn the page. Those marvelously fuzzy bunnies won't sell refrigerators or sports cars, and those risqué cartoons would never fly in the newspaper!

Agencies want to see how you solve visual

HIRED GUN

Bill Mayer states unequivocally, "The number one reason to be in business is to make money. If you're not independently wealthy or have values left over from the sixties, which is not entirely bad, then you're going to have to make a living. For me, freelancing is a marvelous way to do just that—*to make a lot of money!* I am in the business to create art for profit.

"I went to Ringling School of Art. Before I even graduated, I started looking for a job and landed one in a studio."

Mayer unabashedly says, "A freelancer is nothing more than a hired gun. If you're good, with a little marketing you're going to stay busy."

This gunslinger prides himself on his versatility. "The most important thing to do is to concentrate on a standard of excellence and keep it up," Mayer says emphatically. "It doesn't matter which medium you work in. I like working in all of them," he observes. "I get bored with doing one style all the time. I feel by doing many different styles I will be available for many more projects."

His forthright attitude toward selling his work has served Mayer well in discussing business. "I have never had problems talking or negotiating prices," he tells us. "Working with people in general is one of the enjoyable parts of freelancing for me. They're all great people, and I have made a lot of very good friends around the country." But how about those folks not as comfortable or skilled? "Those people who are shy or just don't want to fool with selling themselves can find good reliable people to sell for you."

Mayer advises aspiring illustrators to master basic drawing skills before selling their work. He says, "The art schools offer good basic skills vital to illustrators in this competitive business environment; work on your drawing, design, and color. These foundations are essential to your career."

Mayer outlines an after-school plan. "So, now you're an illustrator. Get yourself out there and show your stuff. Locate your Yellow Pages; look up advertising agencies—it's right before advertising novelties. Go to the first name on the list and call them. Tell them you're putting together a mailing list and you would like to have the names of all of the art directors/creative directors in the agency. You've now got a start on a mailing list. Of course, you can supplement your list with the mailing list of your local art directors' club, which probably can be purchased.

"Now do a self-promotion piece. Flashy posters get a lot of attention when opened, but few make the wall. Try to keep the pieces small—they're cheaper to produce and easier for art directors to file for reference. A little creativity never hurts. Hopefully, you remembered to put your name on it, too!"

What about that portfolio? Mayer says, "Your book is an important reflection on how your work will be perceived by art buyers, art directors, or creative directors. It must be uniformly presented, look professional, and be clean.

"Try to put in only excellent artwork." Mayer cautions, "The number of pieces is not as important as quality. A lot of agencies have drop-off policies, but it is always preferable to meet them in person."

At the review, Mayer says, "Give them a good firm handshake, look them in the eyes, and just be yourself. Most of the time your work should sell itself. Answer any questions, but remember you're not a car salesman. Have some promotional material you can leave, and go on to the next name on your list."

Mayer recommends that beginning illustrators pursue magazines and newspapers as markets that "will give you a lot of freedom to do conceptual and maybe experimental work. The budgets are much lower, but you will get some good exposure (free advertising) in the publications. Make a list of these from the inside credits found in the front of all magazines. Compile and add these to your advertising lists."

Bill Mayer's "Dogfish" was originally an editorial spot for *Adweek*. While delighting the original client, the illustration subsequently was accepted in several competitions, winning a Silver Funny Bone in the Society of Illustrator's Humor show.

Wishing to use the piece as self-promotion, Mayer submitted "Dogfish" as the visual for his ad in the 1989 *American Illustration Showcase*. Upon review, the editors of the annual approached him about employing the image as the cover illustration for the book itself.

When the editors learned that the drawing was used elsewhere, they asked if other imag-ery was available, and the Decatur, Georgia, artist submitted his flamboyant visual for "Conexion '87."

Mayer's illustration was commissioned for a trade show, and was, in its original incarnation, somewhat tame. However, when numerous sketches were not approved, Bill decided to present a much wilder image, thinking he could easily live with the kill fee that would result. The client loved it.

"Conexion" was adapted for the cover of the 1989 edition of *American Showcase*, while "Dogfish" graces his page within the directory. Reprints of "Dogfish" are used as a sample of current work.

© Bill Mayer. Used with permission.

© Bill Mayer. Used with permission.

problems, so if your imagery is somehow pertinent to this demanding market, some card samples might be included in your package. Better still, show that the same imagery developed as a full-blown ad in context with type will meet the real needs of an agency's clients.

LOCAL TALENT

Q. *Do agencies prefer to work with local talent?*

A. In advertising, time is of the essence. Local talent will be preferred, especially if you're needed on a regular basis or to meet tight deadlines. Often, an agency's freelance assignments develop very quickly. Art directors soon get to know who's good, who's dedicated, who's reliable, and who's available.

BUY-OUTS AND WORK-FOR-HIRE

Q. *What is a buy-out? What is work made for hire?*

A. Buy-outs are frequently requested in advertising and greeting card work. In a buy-out, the client, instead of you, will control the fruit of your vision and energies; the client determines how, when, where, and how often your illustration can be used. If the original art is acquired as part of a buy-out, you've forfeited any rights of ownership. There is no subsequent compensation for the continued printed use of your image and you'll have no say in the fate of the actual piece. The buyer owns all reproduction rights and can exploit his property as he sees fit.

Obviously, it's better for the artist to sell limited rights only. Evaluate what the client truly needs and base negotiations on this determination. Original art, if sold, should be a separate transaction. When you create artwork, your ownership of the physical work is immediately established along with your ownership of rights. Buyer or seller should not assume that the sale of rights and originals is a package deal.

If you can't negotiate out of a buy-out, and the client insists on owning all rights despite your best efforts to sell only the rights that are needed, you can: 1. Say "no thank you" and be prepared to walk away from a bad deal; 2. Ac-

cept a trade off, if you can live with it and if it's to your advantage for the future. Is it a good credit to have? A great vehicle for your work? Will it be a dynamite portfolio piece? Is it an entry into a new market? 3. Make it worth your while. A good rule of thumb to remember is that the more you sell, the higher the sale should be. Price accordingly and with prejudice.

The artist should beware of the circumstance known as work made for hire. In a nutshell—*and in the eyes of the copyright law*—the illustrator laboring under a work-for-hire contract effectively becomes an employee without any employee benefits. As the creative's employer the client owns the art and controls the copyright. This is unfair at best, but perfectly legal. The work-for-hire provision robs artists of their just due and is definitely a worst-case scenario. These contracts should be avoided at all costs.

This is the real world, however, and if your baby is down to her last diaper just when you're offered a work-for-hire contract, you may understandably be tempted to accept. I would never preach to, or condemn, those artists who accept these deals. Don't rally behind a cause if you can't reasonably justify the principle. Just know what you're getting into, and accept the consequences of your decision in the light of your situation.

For practical consultation regarding standards and practices, *The Graphic Artists Guild Handbook of Pricing and Ethical Guidelines* should be on every artist's bookshelf. Also consult Tad Crawford's *Legal Guide for the Visual Artist,* plus *The Artist's Friendly Legal Guide* (North Light Books).

ORGANIZATIONS

Q. *What organizations are there for people in the advertising world that would be helpful for a freelancer to join?*

A. On a national level, most large cities have local chapters of The National Advertising Federation, The American Marketing Association, or American Institute of Graphic Arts (AIGA). The Graphic Artists Guild has chapters across the country, and many cities of modest size have an advertising club, art center, or art forum.

CHAPTER SEVEN
CHECKLISTS

An advertising agency:
- ☐ Solves marketing problems by graphic communication.
- ☐ Develops printed matter, audio, and audiovisual materials.
- ☐ Creates copy and appropriate graphics for magazines and newspapers.
- ☐ Produces radio and television commercials.
- ☐ Conceives billboards and direct mail campaigns.
- ☐ Produces literature, sales brochures, and collateral material.
- ☐ Conducts market research and public relations.

Skills advertising agencies call for:
- ☐ Keyline and mechanicals.
- ☐ Model building.
- ☐ Illustration of all types, in all media.
- ☐ Design and production needs.
- ☐ Desktop publishing.

How to find agencies that best suit your talents:
- ☐ Get as much background information as you can through networking and research.
- ☐ Call the agencies and ask: "What are your specialties? Can/do you use freelancers? In what capacity?"
- ☐ Be persistent, be polite, be positive.
- ☐ Schedule a portfolio review.
- ☐ Ask to see their book.

Contacts to develop in advertising:
- ☐ The creative director, the art director.
- ☐ Artists (both staff and freelance).
- ☐ Copy chiefs.
- ☐ Copywriters.

The best way to break into this market:
- ☐ Start as a comp artist.
- ☐ Get referrals.
- ☐ Make sales calls.
- ☐ Skill levels must be high.
- ☐ Join associations such as AIGA or your local art directors club.
- ☐ Promote yourself aggressively.
- ☐ Educate yourself about the market.
- ☐ Maintain contacts and demonstrate your eagerness.

Directories that list advertising agencies:
- ☐ *Standard Directory of Advertising Agencies.*
- ☐ *Artist's Market.*
- ☐ *Madison Avenue Handbook.*
- ☐ Chamber of commerce.
- ☐ Better Business Bureau.
- ☐ Your ad club's members' directory.
- ☐ Local or regional Business-to-Business Yellow Pages.

Organizations to join:
- ☐ National Advertising Federation.
- ☐ The American Marketing Association.
- ☐ American Institute of Graphic Arts (AIGA).
- ☐ The Graphic Artists Guild.
- ☐ Your local advertising club, art center, or art forum.

CHAPTER 8

HOW DO YOU SELL WORK
TO BOOK PUBLISHERS?

TRADE VS. TEXTBOOK

Q. *What's the difference between trade books and textbooks?*

A. According to *The Bookman's* glossary, trade books are "books intended for the general public, and marketed through the bookstores and to libraries, as distinct from textbooks, subscription books, etc." A textbook is "a book used for the study of a particular subject; a manual of instruction."

Sold at retail and appealing to a select audience, trade books can be scholarly works or professional titles, special interest books, instructional manuals, biographies, serious fiction, larger format books, cookbooks, and juveniles (often, but not necessarily with a teaching motive).

Textbooks are educational materials, sold directly to educational institutions.

MASS MARKET BOOK

Q. *What's a mass market book?*

A. Sold at newsstands or bookstores and other retail outlets, and produced in high volume at less cost (to hopefully generate big sales), mass market books are created to appeal to a large audience. Mysteries, spy novels, gothics, fantasy and science fiction, and historical and modern romance novels all fall into this category. Mass market books normally pay higher fees because of larger print runs.

HOUSE DEFINED

Q. *What is a "house"?*

A. A publishing organization, with its various imprints and divisions is called a "house." Several different companies may be found under the central umbrella of a publishing house. For example, take the fictional house of Caputo and Daughters, Inc. (C and D). This Pittsburgh company, in business since 1955, owns a number of imprints. These subsidiaries publish a wide variety of books covering diverse topics.

C and D itself has many divisions, publishing everything from textbooks to adult fiction. Cooper Books, one of its imprints, is an Ohio company specializing only in children's books.

HOUSE HUNTING

Q. *How do you find what type of a book a house publishes? Then how do you find those publishers that best suit your talents?*

A. Haunt the library and the bookstore. Call a publisher and request a catalog. Look for work you like — chances are, if you like their work, they'll like yours. Locate an address on a first or last page, dig up a phone number to get the art director's name, and mail him or her your promotional pieces.

If your information is sketchy, refer to directories such as the *Literary Market Place, Writer's Market, Short Story and Novel Writer's Market,* or *Artist's Market,* to get names, addresses, and phone numbers. Call the publisher and request a catalog.

You can also check out all the major and minor companies at once by attending the American Booksellers Association (ABA) conference. It's held in May, at a different location every year.

HOW TO INTRODUCE YOURSELF

Q. *What is the best way to break into this market?*

A. Let's assume you've looked at books. You've done your research — patronized the library and the bookstores, browsed the newsstand, visited schools and attended trade exhibits. You've studied covers, interior layouts, internal illustrations, and technical drawings. You've analyzed book design — compared tradebooks and textbooks, children's books and adult titles, plus examined the mass market paperbacks. You've located addresses, names and phone numbers, and are ready to mail your promotional pieces.

What to send? Forward the art director samples of your work to keep on file. Best are printed pieces pertaining to your strength — art directors want to work with specialists. En-

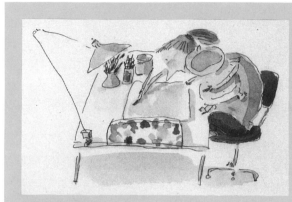

BUILDING A
HEALTHY CAREER

The choice between being a doctor or an illustrator was a difficult one for Laura Cornell of New York City. "While specifically an illustration major at school, I spent very little time with that department. I really disliked it; I didn't know what it was all about. I just knew I'd always wanted to illustrate children's books, but I wasn't actually pursuing that or any aspect of illustration. I was very torn," Cornell admits. But a decision was made, and medicine's loss became illustration's gain.

"The trials and tribulations at the beginning of my career revolved around the nature of freelancing in Los Angeles, a lack of confidence, and living at home immediately after college. Living at home meant no financial pressure. Freelancing in L.A. meant appointments miles apart, entire days consumed coming up with new names and places to show. The lack of printed work—the age-old 'experience wanted, but how do you get the experience if no one will hire you?'—was specifically a problem for me. I was told continually by art directors to go to New York."

And Cornell did. "When I arrived in New York," she says, "I found an entire world of illustration." The New York illustration industry was unfamiliar to her experience and foreign to her mindset. "In New York, it's all spoon-fed—illustration is everywhere. I discovered that anything—fine art, beautiful oil paintings, lithography, or woodcuts—could be considered illustration in New York. There's a certain slickness in L.A., into which I did not fit."

Cornell did not promote herself until about four years ago (roughly seven years after her move to New York City). "I just took my portfolio around, leaving samples behind. It was easy to do here; everything's just about walking distance. I'd pack in lots of portfolio reviews."

Cornell sought out appointments for the first year or two. Thereafter, art directors began calling her, wanting to see her book. "About three years ago I decided there should be a change," Cornell says. "I was content with the work I was getting but felt things were not getting bigger and better, not really progressing. I decided to take out an ad in *American Showcase*, which I did for three consecutive years."

Cornell calls this action "the most valuable thing I've done. The ads bring in long-distance work from design firms and ad agencies—clients with bigger budgets." Illustrating the children's books *Annie Bananie* and *Earl's Too Cool for Me* for Harper & Row, plus works in progress now, were also a result of her first *Showcase* ad.

Cornell enjoys working with book publishers because of the nature of the assignments and the flexibility of the work relationship. "You can have as much or as little contact with the publishing house as you want—specifically the editor with whom you are working. Deadlines are much more flexible, and, best of all, there is almost nil art direction—you can almost do anything you choose.

"When I'm showing my portfolio, book publishers consistently give me some useful and helpful information. They simply say, 'We are interested in seeing a penciled book dummy, either your own story or an existing classic.' They want to see if you can lay out a book. A finished piece does not seem all that important.

"Have a one-style portfolio," Cornell continues. "Being a jack-of-all-trades is easy to do, but a total mistake. An art director must have a clean, simple image of what you do when you leave his office.

"The best advice anyone ever gave me was when an art director, looking over my sketches, asked me, 'Why do you think I called you to do this job? For what you do.' For me that hits everything on the nose."

Laura Cornell's first trade book assignment, *Annie Bananie,* by Leah Komaiko, celebrates the wonderful and wacky relationship of two dear friends. The book's format challenged Cornell. "There was a huge chunk of text that was extremely minimal, and I had to break all this down to fit into a standard thirty-two-page children's book. So, I came up with a variety of images. It was easy and fun for me. I could do whatever I wanted; my editor made very few suggestions, revisions, or corrections—one of the things that was so nice about doing this particular book."

Cornell found the project very satisfying, and *Annie Bananie* has led to additional books for Harper & Row. The illustrator—already busy with her advertising and editorial work, has more children's books in progress, in the planning stages, or pending contract.

© Laura Cornell. Used with permission.

© Laura Cornell. Used with permission.

close a cover letter with your sample package, or make sure an initial brochure highlights your work history. Publishing credits add credibility and parallel experience is a plus (any work that even remotely resembles publishing responsibilities can only help). Follow up with a phone call at some point shortly thereafter. Ask if they'd like to see more samples or suggest a portfolio review.

It breaks down to this: Determine where you fit in, then go for it. Get your marketing and self-promotion in gear, and fine tune your book. Buy a spiffy interview outfit and polish your in-person routine. Work the phones and the mails, then hit the road!

FREELANCE POSSIBILITIES

Q. *Other than books, what do publishers produce that might need freelance help?*

A. Publishers use freelancers for illustration (for jackets and covers, as well as text), design, in production and technical areas (such as layout, paste-up, and book dummying), as photographers, stylists, and model makers.

Publishers also need freelancers to create ads, direct mail and promotional pieces, newsletters, brochures and catalogs, and point-of-purchase displays. Many book publishers also produce activities (coloring books, for instance), educational aids (flash cards), games, and posters that provide illustration opportunities.

You'll find that most publishers use freelance help, especially the larger houses. The easiest way to verify this is to call an art director and ask.

WORKING THROUGH THE MAIL

Q. *Are book publishers open to mailed submissions?*

A. It's probably easier to work long distance with a publisher than with other illustration markets. Most publishers are quite used to working through the mails. Usually, deadlines are reasonable to generous in book publishing, and book projects are typically extended affairs—rarely rushed into, seldom rushed through.

The house publishes many books, and evaluates far more than ever see print. A manuscript may be tied up for two months or more while it is reviewed and evaluated by any number of people, before a decision to publish is made.

Mailed submissions are viewed as the initial phase of the process. Matching the right illustrator with the right project is done thoughtfully and over time, so a mailed submission dovetails right into the work schedule of an extremely careful, but exceedingly busy art director.

JOBS FOR DESIGNERS

Q. *Is there much of a market for book designers? How do you introduce yourself as a designer to book publishers?*

A. There is not a large market in all cities for book designers, but it does exist. However, it might be a bit more difficult to freelance as a designer because publishers may prefer their designers to be local, if not in-house. When they look out of town, the house hires freelancers from the big publishing centers (New York, Boston, and Chicago). These cities employ a lot of book designers, and those folks work with all the major publishers in those areas.

Why? Any designer can design covers, but the interior is a specialized area and requires specific training (often on-the-job). A design studio may create a cover, but it will usually be the specialist—the book designer—who designs the interior. However, a house usually finds it preferable to hire one book designer to do both cover and interior.

To introduce yourself, send samples of pages where typography is a crucial design element, and present this portfolio to appropriate art directors or editors. Obviously, print samples will be best. Bright ideas and enthusiasm will be appreciated, but knowledge and experience are what the publisher needs and demands.

A designer—one with a good education (let's say a BFA with graphic design concentration)—qualifies to be a book designer at an entry level. Publishers will only use freelancers in book design if they have a lot of experience. You may only be able to learn book design by working on staff at a publishing house; otherwise, your design work may be limited to covers.

COLLABORATIVE SUBMISSION

Q. *A friend of mine wants me to illustrate a book, then submit it to a publisher for consideration. Is this the way it's usually done, or am I wasting my time?*

A. Sorry, it doesn't work this way. Don't waste your time or energy, because this isn't the way a potential book is usually welcomed. Suggest that your friend submit the story to the editorial division while you concentrate on the art department.

Publishers prefer to arrange the marriage, so to speak, unless you are both author and artist. Some writers have the clout to demand a certain illustrator, but most publishers will match up a manuscript with their artist of choice. The in-house design process is crucial to a book's final look and ultimate success, so few books are submitted or accepted as a fait accompli, in finished form.

If you're the writer and illustrator, your book should be submitted as a book dummy, accompanied by the manuscript, and one to two samples of the finished art (not the originals, however). If you're an illustrator hoping to land a book project, submit a portfolio that best showcases your style and that will, with luck and some market study, meet the publisher's needs.

SAMPLES

Q. *What type of samples should you send to book publishers?*

A. As with any portfolio sent through the mail, send nonreturnable samples for the files or "expendable" samples you can afford to lose, such as a photocopied book dummy, transparencies, stats, high quality black-and-white or color photocopies, or tearsheets.

A portfolio sent to a book publisher must convey style and technique, plus a few more things:

■ Your work should be a close fit to that of the publisher. A house specializing in technical manuals would simply toss out children's illustration, for example. So keep your samples relevant.

■ Samples should be both black-and-white (line and/or gradated tone) and color. Send full-color art definitely; two- and three-color art, if you have it. Don't send mechanicals, but you're one step ahead in this field if you have experience with hand separation, so include any pre-separated work.

■ Demonstrate solid character development and interaction. Let's see a main character in a variety of moods and emotions, from different angles, in various positions. Show this central figure with others: one-on-one, in small group shots, and large crowd scenes.

■ Vary environments—intimate surroundings, wide-open spaces, diverse weather conditions, in a variety of climates.

■ Think story: Highlight your ability to juggle subject matter, orchestrate action, and communicate a sequence of events.

■ Show that you understand composition and the crucial relationship between type and visuals.

■ Send appropriate samples. You won't find many little duckies on the covers of murder mysteries, or three-headed Martian brain munchers in Mr. Clumsy's Workshop. If you're writing the story, include a rough book dummy. If you don't have printed pieces, write your own tales, or redesign for existing tales, then do book covers and page illustrations for these.

Remember that book publishers don't ask much—only that it's absolutely clear you know how to design and illustrate a book. No sweat, right?

WHOM TO CONTACT

Q. *Whom do you contact, the editor or the art director? In a directory, there is usually more than one editor and more than one art director listed. Which one do you choose?*

A. Research, research, research. Study the directories. If you can't find the person's name, make lots of calls and ask questions. Find out who accepts submissions and ask specifically for that person's name, title (editor, submissions editor, art director?), and department.

The editor probably has more control than the art director. But art directors may be more supportive of your cause. If they like your work, art directors may be easier to deal with than editors. In general, send an art submission to the art director; if you are writing the story too, send your package to the appropriate editor.

LOCAL FIRST?

Q. *It is best to work with a local publisher first, then expand your market?*

A. I always feel it is best to start locally so you can have that person-to-person contact, but it's neither completely necessary nor mandatory. Although unlikely, there may not be a publisher in your area.

Art director Debbie Kokoruda, at Cincinnati's South-Western Publishing Company says, "Publishers may try new or inexperienced people because their accessibility is the trade-off. If you are soliciting your work to publishers all over the country, it should be because you (offer) a lot of experience unavailable to the publisher. It's more difficult to work with out-of-towners, but certainly is common practice in publishing."

DIRECTORIES

Q. *What directories list names of book publishers?*

A. *The Literary Market Place* (LMP), *Artist's Market,* and *Writer's Market* are excellent sources. Also consult the *Publisher's Directory, Short Story and Novel Writer's Market, Children's Writer's Marketplace* and *Children's Writer's and Illustrator's Market.* Write to the Children's Book Council to receive their list of publishers, which includes names of art directors and editors.

ORGANIZATIONS

Q. *What organizations should I join to get to know the people in book publishing?*

A. Try the American Institute of Graphic Art, which has local chapters and national membership, plus an annual Book Show. Look into the Chicago Book Clinic and Book Builders West, which have annual seminars and a Book Show. Again, write to the Children's Book Council. Check out your local art directors club.

TRADE MAGAZINES

Q. *What magazines cover the book publishing industry?*

A. The most popular magazine covering publishing is *Publisher's Weekly.* Also read *The Artist's Magazine* and *Writer's Digest.*

CHAPTER EIGHT CHECKLISTS

Publishers use freelancers for:
☐ Illustration on jackets, covers, and text.
☐ Layout and design.
☐ Production and technical areas.
☐ Photography, and as stylists and model makers.
☐ Advertising, direct mail, and promotional pieces.
☐ Work on newsletters, brochures, and catalogs, plus point-of-purchase displays.
☐ Producing activities, educational aids, games, and posters.

To find what type of book a house publishes:
☐ Visit the library and the bookstore.
☐ Call a publisher and request a catalog.
☐ Look for books you like.
☐ Attend the ABA convention.

Steps in submitting work to a publisher:
☐ Writers should submit stories to the editorial division, while artists should concentrate on the art department; publishers prefer to match up a manuscript with an artist.
☐ Manuscript and dummy should be accompanied by copies of one or two pieces of finished art.
☐ Submit a portfolio that best showcases your style.

Samples sent to book publishers should:
☐ Be nonreturnable, for the art director's files.

☐ Be expendable—a photocopied book dummy, transparencies, stats, high quality black-and-white or color photocopies, or tearsheets.
☐ Convey style and technique.
☐ Include both black and white and color.
☐ Demonstrate solid character development and interaction.
☐ Vary environments, subject matter, mood, and emotion.
☐ Highlight your ability to orchestrate action and communicate a sequence of events.
☐ Show that you understand composition.
☐ Show that you understand the relationship between type and visuals by sending samples of pages designed with typography as a crucial design element.
☐ Be sure your samples could illustrate the types of books the house publishes.

Directories that list names of book publishers:
☐ *The Literary Market Place* (LMP).
☐ *Artist's Market.*
☐ *Writer's Market.*
☐ *The Children's Writer's Marketplace.*
☐ *Children's Writer's and Illustrator's Market.*
☐ *Short Story and Novel Writer's Market.*
☐ *Publisher's Directory.*

Organizations to join or consult:
☐ American Institute of Graphic Art.
☐ Chicago Book Clinic.
☐ Book Builders West.
☐ Your local art directors club.
☐ Children's Book Council.

Magazines to read:
☐ *Publisher's Weekly.*
☐ *The Artist's Magazine.*
☐ *Writer's Digest.*

CHAPTER 9

HOW DO YOU SELL WORK TO GREETING CARD COMPANIES?

GREETING CARD DESIGN

Q. *Greeting card companies say they buy "designs." Is a design the same as an illustration?*

A. In the greeting card industry, a design is essentially the same as an illustration. A design is the idea (or concept) and the illustration is the finished product. The term design refers to the visual element that accompanies the editorial (the copy) on a card. This artwork is used for a single purpose—a select card or one page or individual spread in a booklet or calendar. The design may be a basic character study, a particular scene, or a still life. It could be an abstract composition, a simple pattern or border, or perhaps a concept composed entirely of calligraphy or type.

Any medium can be used for a card design. You'll find designs done in pen or pencil, water media (including acrylics and gouache), cut paper or fabric collage, and embroidery. A design could also be paper or clay construction, or hand-tinted photography. It could even be done entirely in what is termed "finishes"— gold leaf, die cuts, embossing, etc.

COMPANY RESEARCH

Q. *How does a greeting card company choose the cards it will publish?*

A. A card company targets production to selected markets, such as the young and trendy in specialty shops or the generally middle-class shoppers at the drugstore. Keeping a deliberate finger on the pulse of current popular culture, card and paper product companies do extensive market research to determine what categories of cards the public wants to send. Pre-market testing determines which visual styles and messages the buying public prefers.

TYPES OF CARDS

Q. *What types of cards are there?*

A. Basically, card companies produce two types: occasion cards for standard holidays and established events (such as birthdays, graduations, anniversaries, friendship, sym-
pathy), and non-occasion or everyday cards.

Within these two primary lines, look for these general categories: traditional (an established, long accepted, and rather realistic approach); studio (contemporary and sophisticated, with biting wit); humorous (also funny, but usually simpler and not as caustic; leaning toward the cartoon); romantic (hearts and flowers, decidedly sentimental); juvenile (appealing to children); cute (adorable characters in charming situations); and stylish (a chic, modern look).

ALTERNATIVE CARDS

Q. *What are alternative cards?*

A. For a company to sell more products, their cards must reflect contemporary subject matter and topics of special interest to the card buyer. Current trends and the lifestyle changes American consumers have made over the last decade dictated the development of a new genre that stretched the parameters and attacked the old taboos: the alternative card.

Almost every company now markets so-called alternative cards, so it's safe to say that the label is somewhat inoperative. Thanks to the alternative card phenomenon, it's not unusual now to see cards dealing with women's rights, divorce, remarriage and the extended family, the singles scene, or alternative sexual preferences. There are even cards for dieting, congratulations on your promotion, pet death, computers, high (or low) finance, and coping with everything from poor service to retirement. If the subject is relevant and current, chances are you'll now find a card addressing the situation.

You'll still find the "warm and fuzzy" cards, carrying cuddly copy or bubbly messages, but today's product lines approach subject matter with new sensibilities. Modern cards also act as small doses of psychotherapy, delivering sensitive counseling or gentle expressions of advice, support, and concern. But, look out— cards these days are also rife with sly wit, biting sarcasm, and decidedly offbeat (even downright wacky) humor. They may make you

MOPPING UP WITH THE MUPPETS

"When I graduated from college, I had never even heard of a portfolio," says Dallas illustrator Mary Grace Eubank. "I had excellent grades, but the people at my first job interview could not have cared less about honors or grades or anything. They wanted to see a portfolio, and I didn't even know what they were talking about.

"I went back over to the dean and asked 'What is a portfolio?' He gave me some advice and I basically put my book together at home.

"If I had it to do over again I think I would have gone to a commercial art school. I think it's much more concentrated study, and you are exposed to more tricks of the trade. There's a lot of respect in the professional field for certain art schools."

After graduation, Eubank worked for Susan Crane Packaging in Dallas. "I started out doing mainly scheduling," she remembers, "which had little to do with artwork. It was more of a secretarial thing, although I was labeled a designer. I didn't do much at first, but it was a wonderful beginning. Like osmosis, you absorb the talent around you—and there was a lot of talent at Susan Crane, plus a lot of freedom."

Eubank worked there for a year and a half, stopping, she says, "to have babies."

But she continued to freelance for the company. Divorced in 1976, Eubank tells us, "I freelanced for a while, but it was real shaky. I had two children to support, I was living month to month, and I needed a steady income I could count on."

So, Eubank began working full-time, doing giftwrap and greeting card design for Drawing Board Greeting Cards. "Not much finished work—mostly design," she recalls. "My freelancing was not stable enough for me, but I did have a little bit of outside income."

During her tenure at Drawing Board, the company landed a contract to license the Muppets for greeting cards and calendars. Thus, Eubank began designing for Sesame Street.

Eubank explains how she got the job: "Children's Television Workshop had an illustrator they used through New York, which was the only way they'd operate. We would send the designs to them, they would send it to the illustrator, and then Drawing Board would produce it. Right before the New York Stationery Show, there was a problem with the illustrator. Nothing was ready on time and everybody panicked, so they agreed to let me go ahead and do the finish—a major coup, because they just don't work that way.

"My finishes were primarily studio cards back then—the tall, skinny cards with the funny gag lines. Going into Muppets was a little bit different for me. They're puffier and cuter and my style was a little more cartoonish."

Eubank enjoyed the assignment and the prestige of having a client like CTW. "The problem was I couldn't go to work for them directly as long as I was working for Drawing Board. That's when the big decision came whether or not to freelance again. I was afraid to get back into it—what would I do if I couldn't make it one month? I decided I would go out on my own when I had one year's salary in the bank, and at least one outside client on a contract basis."

When Eubank did make the jump, she only had one month's salary in the bank, plus an outside contract with Texas Instruments to produce a series of twenty books to accompany educational toys. "Steady income for at least year," Eubank points out. "I had remarried, so there was a bit more security. I made the big move, but it

Mary Grace Eubank had sent a number of promotional pieces to Current with no success. In fact, a portfolio was returned with regrets two years before she was called "out of the blue" to work on a variety of small jobs for the Colorado-based mail-order company. Steady work led to this assignment, one of twelve illustrations for Current's 1990 "Sheep Thrills" Calendar. Eubank intends to use the calendar as a holiday gift promotion, as her introduction to prospective art buyers (or a reminder to an existing client), and as part of sample packages sent upon request.

took a lot of courage."

Eubank found working for Sesame Street not only lucrative, but a tremendous springboard as well. "Because they license to major companies, I'd be working directly with the art directors and developing our relationship." When she experienced "Big Bird burnout" a few years ago, Eubank says, "I was amazed and delighted at the response when I contacted the company for non-Muppet jobs.

"Now, I still do a few Muppet jobs. The bulk of my work has gone into a more 'generic' area. These jobs are much more fun—you can do your own characters, there's a lot more freedom. But I like to stay connected with Sesame Street. I was real lucky. It's a matter of being in the right place at the right time, and I give CTW a lot of credit for enabling me to work for the people I work for now."

Eubank remembers her early trials and tribulations all too well. "The insecurity of the whole thing, having two small children and taking my credit very seriously—I would just get so upset if I couldn't pay a bill. Freelancing requires so much self-discipline. Suddenly it was up to me to make these decisions—to get up and get there and to work all day, to not put things off and to not procrastinate. That's the deadliest sin of freelancing: the procrastination bug.

"Every time you do an illustration your ego is on the line. It's part of you; it's something you created. When it's rejected, it's really difficult to keep in mind that it's not you, it's that piece of art that's being rejected. You develop confidence, but in the beginning it's very difficult. I had a hard time with that."

Eubank recently discovered how self-promotion can expand an artist's horizons. "I did little self-promotion until a few years ago. I was in an art supply store and found the *American Showcase*. I had no idea what it was, but I enjoyed the art, and finally, after looking at it several times, realized you could buy a page in the thing. Anyone who wanted to spend the money

This 1985 greeting card sample was done for Drawing Board Greeting Cards. It's just one assignment—out of what Eubank "guesstimates" to be in the hundreds—that continued Eubank's freelance relationship with her former full-time employer (now Carlton Cards). Four years later, the successful card has been reprinted.

© Mary Grace Eubank. Used with permission.

could be in the book. I could be in that book.

"That very same month I went to New York and attended a Graphic Artists Guild meeting. The topic was self-promotion. They emphasized so strongly how important it was to spend at least 10 percent of your income a year promoting yourself and sending things out. I had never done this before. So I decided to do a page in the *Showcase*. One week after the book came out, I got a job for Wendy's that paid for the ad three times over.

"You receive two thousand copies of your page. It's nicely printed and the color is good, so you have a composite piece to send to people. I sent out about thirty or forty pieces, primarily to publishing houses. It worked really well.

"Most of the art directors I work with are out of the city, so I've developed a telephone relationship with them. I have several art directors whom I see when I go to New York. When I started freelancing and everything was on my tab, I thought I couldn't afford to go to New York, and I didn't go for a couple of years. The first year that I went, it really paid off.

"It's important to utilize every minute you're there. I usually try to go during the New York Stationery Show. I plan as many

meetings as I can. I schedule interviews, take my portfolio around to publishing houses. I try to take someone to lunch or to the theater. Schmoozing pays off.

"I'm very direct with the people I am romancing and they know exactly why I'm there—you *can* develop a friendship and still help each other.

"It wasn't until I got that page in the *Showcase* that I attracted some Texas clients. It's just as easy for me to mail something to Ft. Worth as it is to New York, but the local clients seem to think you should be there in person. However, I don't really care where anybody is as long as the projects are fun and the pay is good."

Eubank advises beginning freelancers to be solid professionals. "Exercise discipline. Don't procrastinate. Be reliable about deadlines—this gives you a real advantage, so work on that. I take deadlines very seriously," says Eubank. "It's rare that I call an art director with excuses. Sometimes if I'm going to be a day or two late, I'll call—but I'll work a lot of midnight hours and weekends before I'll do that."

In closing, she comments, "Every year you'll get better. When you're starting out you're just beginning to exercise your potential—you don't know where you're going to be in ten years."

blush, and you'll read language previously found only in grafitti.

SUITABLE ART

Q. *Are different types of art preferred for different types of cards?*

A. The greeting (often called the sentiment) in a card defines the art and of course, vice versa. Different art styles are preferred for different types of cards. Think of Gary Larsen's "The Far Side" done by Norman Rockwell and you'll easily get the point.

A card company must consider its entire card line when choosing what to publish. The aim is to achieve an overall stylistic balance, both visual and editorial, throughout the product line. Visually, you will find a range of the highly traditional to the very hip, and a great variety of art styles and media.

The trendiest, most avant-garde or ultra-sophisticated modes may not be incorporated into a product line, however. Subject matter (for example, unicorns or teddy bears), a particular style (the currently popular minimal drawing approach), or fresh technique (the airbrush) must prove to be more than a fad to be considered for the line. Greeting card art directors and designers often look to the fashion and interior design markets to gauge the success of an available look or theme, or even of a color palette.

Only small card companies can afford to be on the cutting edge of new trends. A smaller card line means shorter lead times in preparing product. This translates into a much slighter financial risk should a fad prove short-lived. Because of this advantage, these small mavericks set the pace for the industry at large.

RESEARCHING CARDS

Q. *How can I research what type of cards a company produces?*

A. Your first stop will be the local card and gift marts. Go to every shop you see (some franchises carry one company exclusively, but most stores carry lines from many different companies). Spend lots of time at the card racks, researching the types of cards each company produces. Buy the cards you like best and that seem closely related to your own style. Check logos and get a feel for which companies produce the kind of cards that most appeal to you.

If you're not buying today, jot down company data while browsing—but always clear it with the clerk or owner at some point. You won't have any trouble if you just introduce yourself, state your purpose, and express a small bit of thanks. Oh, yes—bring a pad and pencil—don't borrow envelopes for note paper!

If you can't find a particular company's wares, call them and ask where to find their cards in your area. You could also write to the company's creative department and request a current catalog along with artists' guidelines for submissions. Use your letterhead and enclose a business card, so they have reasonable assurance you're not a spy for the competition.

To research virtually all the greeting card companies at once, attend the New York Stationery Show, held in May at the Jacob Javits Convention Center. Here you can interview and show your portfolio, market and promote your work, network, and examine every aspect of every company—all at one time, under one roof.

OTHER PAPER PRODUCTS

Q. *Do most greeting card companies also produce other paper products such as stationery and note cards? Are these also good markets?*

A. Most card companies of any size also produce note cards, stationery, party goods, and giftwrap. For example, Exyzee Greetings—a hypothetical company—must offer their card shops a complete line of paper products and be able to fill all the product space in the shop. If Exyzee only makes cards, the stores they service will have to buy other merchandise from the competition, who we'll call Abeecee Designs. If Abeecee also produces cards, they will be more likely to snatch a larger share of the card shop trade.

While freelancers are not used as frequently

WORKING ON BOTH SIDES OF THE FENCE

Mary Thelen has worked both sides of the fence in greeting cards—as an art director and as a freelance illustrator/designer. Her tenure on staff has helped her become a more competent freelancer. Aware of all stages of production, Thelen understands what is demanded of each person involved, every step along the way.

One of Thelen's early jobs was as an art director's assistant at Hallmark. "With the opportunity to roam the department, I helped anyone who needed an extra pair of hands. I received illustration assignments, though my job description was focused on getting other people's art through production. I learned to operate all the equipment in the photo lab and worked with a first-rate print shop. I was a color stylist sometimes (color stylists develop the color palette according to trends and add color to the artwork), and had unlimited use of a terrific visual reference library. Free art supplies, contact with a staff of five hundred highly skilled illustrators to learn from—all this in an environment equipped with state-of-the-art technical facilities. It was like a two-year internship."

Thelen recommends taking a job at a greeting card company in order to learn the business thoroughly. "Most of us need the additional education, the seasoning attained by working at a regular job among colleagues who are more experienced. It's the best way to get the big picture. I also advise students to seek as much small-time freelance work as they can get while in school—campus publication, ads for local merchants or nonprofit organizations. Pay is inconsequential; what counts is if it gets printed. If you can show your successful solutions to real-world design problems, someone will bank on your skills as an artist."

After working with Hallmark, Thelen was an art director at Abbey Press. She then worked at a design studio, learning production skills. From there she freelanced with ad agencies and book publishers, while illustrating ads for a few local businesses. "This was a whole new level of freelance experience. Lots of cold calls (the hardest part), and lots of schlepping my portfolio around town. I learned that agency art directors have a different attitude than greeting card art directors. They are more aggressive and less tolerant. Because they work with much tighter deadlines, they're under an entirely different kind of stress.

"I would come to them with a portfolio full of greeting card and original illustrations, and they'd say, 'You have beautiful work, but how could we use it? We need to see these illustrations in the context of an ad, with type.' At the time I thought, 'What's wrong with these doodahs? They're art directors; it's their job to visualize how a particular style would fit into their work.' But their suggestion to put my illustrations into an ad format was one of the best pieces of advice I ever got, and it was free. It's important to research what art directors want to see. It saves you work and lets you know where you should put in the extra effort."

The best advice Thelen can give to other freelancers is to develop a good working relationship with clients. "It helps if you love your clients," she affirms. "After all, they're putting food on your table. They just bought you that neat outfit or that new car. If you can be genuinely concerned about the well-being of the people you work with, you'll get their love and respect in return. And people like to give work to people they love and respect."

© Mary K. Thelen. Used with permission.

The next time your date is old enough to have invented the airplane, just make the best of it.

He may be Mister Wright.

© Mary K. Thelen. Used with permission.

I hear you like to do STRANGE things on your BiRTHDAY..

Why doesn't that surprise me?

Mary Thelen, of Dallas, Texas, was an art director at Carlton Cards for five years. She continued to maintain a freelance relationship with her former full-time employer, resulting in this assignment for the company. "Mister Wright" is one element of a twenty-card promotion relating to the contemporary working woman. Thelen developed a fresh concept to fit existing copy, and a successful presentation won her the job.

When sending sample packages to prospective art buyers, Thelen purposely bundles several pieces from a selection of promotions to show a versatility of style—her bouncy cut-paper technique is showcased in this card for Argus Communications. Showing several such pieces also demonstrates that she can develop a number of images that hang together as a group, with each having an individual punch—a consistency of theme coupled with a variety of visual characteristics.

on these other paper product lines, there are companies that specialize in stationery and note cards, giftwrap, or party goods. These may be better outlets for your art.

USING FREELANCE HELP

Q. *How can you tell if a greeting card company uses freelance talent?*

A. Generally, small companies use more freelancers because their output can't support an ample or full-time art staff. But many small companies are one-person operations. There are also complaints that small companies don't pay as well and may not pay promptly.

Large companies use fewer freelancers because they have extensive in-house art staffs. If your style is notably unique, you may get the nod for a particular job, but you could indeed be viewed as the proverbial "little fish in the big pond." When you work with the giants, size does not always equate with job opportunities or harmonious relationships, and the red tape can be particularly frustrating.

The medium-size competitor is probably your most dependable and reliable source. Since they're slugging it out with the big guys in certain product areas, these mid-range companies have busy staffs. They actively welcome and court outside help—card designs are always changing and the demand for new art, plus the desire for a variety of looks, is often more than the in-house staff can handle.

The greeting card industry has a voracious appetite for bright ideas and innovative styles. According to the Greeting Card Association in Washington, D.C., greeting card publishing is the largest user of creative talent next to advertising, and freelancers are considered the fresh air that keeps the card industry breathing.

One way to gauge the size and dependability of a card company is by reading their listing in the annual *Artist's Market.* Card companies that don't have a listing here are not likely to need much freelance help. Another simple way is to call the company. Ask for the personnel office or creative department, and ask directly: "Do you use freelancers? To whom do I send my samples? Would you please send artist's guidelines for submission?"

SAMPLES

Q. *What do I send as initial samples?*

A. Send work that demonstrates your excellent drawing ability, a good color and design sense, plus the superior technique you've honed to perfection.

Send imagery appropriate to cards (and you've determined this by exhaustive research, right?). The only inappropriate samples are those irrelevant to this field. Let's say you do airbrush, which is often used in greeting cards. If all your airbrush samples are illustrations of engines and machinery, don't expect many assignments from a greeting card company. If your art style, wit, and personality are suited to greeting card work, it shouldn't be a big chore to determine which of your samples are appropriate to send.

Print samples are a plus. Send slides, tearsheets, or color photocopies (again—don't send the originals). A few cards are done in black and white, so black-and-white samples are okay for showing line work, but you really need to present color! Samples of mechanicals are not really helpful, unless you're applying for a position in the production art department (a crucial part of any card company, by the way).

Busy art directors need to get a sense of your style and skill. They don't have a lot of time to view portfolios, chat on the phone, or to return samples sent without sufficient return postage. Don't make the unreasonable request that the card company insure the return package.

Often an art director will make copies for the files, but it's best to send samples he or she can keep. If you want something back, say so and include as SASE. Make sure you follow through with periodic updates.

VERSE OR NO VERSE?

Q. *Should artists write verse on their initial samples?*

A. Remember, you are a visual artist. Art directors do not buy copy; editors do not buy art. Verse or copy on artwork is not necessary, unless you're also selling yourself as a wordsmith. If you are talented with text and wish to

NURTURING AN INDEPENDENT SPIRIT

Formerly a staff artist at a record company, Jennifer Berman has taken matters into her own hands. Under the banner of her own company, Humerus Cartoons, the Chicago illustrator creates her line of postcards and related merchandise and distributes them nationally.

An independent spirit moved Berman to set out on her own. About five years ago, she moved to Berkeley, California, after graduating from Antioch College. She decided to work for a year before starting law school. "I got a job in an office and *hated* it."

Three months was all Berman could handle and, with the little money she saved, she quit the office scene. "I don't know what possessed me, but I printed up sixteen postcards. And I did it all the wrong way—the paper was bad, the printer wasn't right—I had no idea what I was doing. But I knew that anything would be better than working in an office. So I talked to some street vendors and decided to set up a booth on Telegraph Avenue, selling postcards."

During the year Berman sold her cards this way, she received some pivotal education. "I took two great courses that offered a wealth of knowledge. One class dealt with the marketing and design of greeting cards, and the other was on humorous writing and illustration. Taking these courses shaved off years of struggling to figure out how to do it on your own. Thanks to these classes I've ended up both selling my cartoons to magazines, newspapers, and card companies and also forming my own card company."

How do you distribute and sell cards nationally? "There are certain events you cannot miss, and one of them is the New York Stationery Show," Berman points out. "There you meet reps who sell to specific geographical areas. They sell the cards for you. A rep gets you the orders, and you fill the orders. I market my work in Chicago, but my reps are my national sales fleet."

Since she recently set out on her own, Berman knows the ups and downs of freelancing. "The bad news may be that we're never sure how the bills get paid, but the good news is that life is an adventure. The Taoist philosopher Lao Tsu was the first to come up with the concept of 'going with the flow,' meaning don't dwell on the negative—turn your disappointments into lessons. While you're forging your path, you'll meet interesting people, you'll learn some neat stuff, and you will eventually become financially secure."

This is one of Berman's cartoon postcards, which she creates and markets herself locally. Contacts made at the annual New York Stationery Show take care of the rest of the country.

© 1989 Jennifer Berman.

be considered as a writer, make this clear in your cover letter and include verse suggestions with your package.

COMMISSIONED DESIGNS

Q. *Do greeting card companies buy mailed submissions or do they usually commission a design?*

A. Card companies are open to mailed submissions, but marketing your concepts can be a very tough sell (and marketing those bright ideas alone is not prudent).

Designs are usually commissioned by card companies as opposed to being bought over the transom. Company policies may vary, of course, so check with each. Every company has an individual philosophy and program, every studio has their own way of doing things, so don't create finished art and try to sell it for publication.

You may have a great concept for a card, but that doesn't mean it will fit the requirements of the product lines currently being assigned. Will a card be full color, two color or three color? Will it be scanned or mechanically separated? Does a design incorporate special processes like foil stamping, multiple folds, die cuts or embossing? These choices are determined by the production budget allotted to a particular line.

Actively pursue the commission work and continue to develop and present your designs; this will be the fruitful path to success without undue heartache. Once you've established a track record with a certain studio, it's a different story. The company might solicit submissions and may even offer a contract guaranteeing a certain minimum purchase.

SELLING ALL RIGHTS

Q. *Should I sell all rights to my design or negotiate for royalties?*

A. According to Ms. Marty Roelandt, an experienced greeting card art director, it's not uncommon for card companies to purchase all rights to designs. Card designs are invariably done quickly and in volume. They have little marketability in other areas and you can't usually sell an old design to another company. Unless you have a unique character, concept, or a style that is well-known, expect to sell your card designs outright to some companies. Also keep in mind that royalties on a single design may add up to less than an outright sale.

CARD FORMAT

Q. *Should I send vertical or horizontal designs?*

A. At one time the vertical card had more "rack appeal" because the vertical format displayed captions most clearly. But, with modern plexiglass display cases, layout is now simply a matter of company preference. Consult individual artist's guidelines for this information.

Most designs used today are vertical, but you will see horizontals. Don't worry too much about sending things in a card format unless you have printed samples of cards done for other clients. If you've got the right look for the line, an art director will direct you on the specifics when you get an assignment.

If you have decided to send mock-ups, they should be designed with the caption in mind. No matter what the format, design around the part of the card that will show in the display; this top third is important and must look particularly attractive.

STANDARD SIZE

Q. *What is the standard size of a greeting card?*

A. Sizes vary. There is no standard for the industry. Submission guidelines will instruct you as to that company's size specifications and requirements. In general, it will be in proportions similar to a 5″ × 7″ format.

CHAPTER NINE
CHECKLISTS

When you're researching types of cards:
- ☐ Visit your local card and gift marts.
- ☐ Buy the cards that best relate to you and your own style.
- ☐ Check logos to see which companies produce your favorites.
- ☐ Jot down company data while browsing.
- ☐ Call the company or write to the company's creative department to request a current catalog and artists' guidelines for submissions.
- ☐ Attend the New York Stationery Show.

When sending your initial samples:
- ☐ Send work that demonstrates a sense of your style and skill, drawing ability, color and design sense, plus technique.
- ☐ Send imagery appropriate to the company's line of cards.
- ☐ If possible, include print samples.
- ☐ Send slides, tearsheets, or color photocopies.
- ☐ Show color.
- ☐ Send samples that the art director can keep or enclose a SASE for return of your material.
- ☐ Don't send verse unless you're also selling yourself as a writer.
- ☐ Don't create finished art and try to sell it for publication.
- ☐ Most designs are vertical, but either vertical or horizontal designs are okay—consult individual artists' guidelines.
- ☐ Proportions on samples should be similar to a 5"×7" format.

To research trends that influence greeting cards:
- ☐ Look at fashion, advertising, home decoration and furnishings.
- ☐ Study current design, graphics, color, and pattern.
- ☐ Watch television.
- ☐ Read for both news and entertainment, business and pleasure—especially read lots of women's magazines since the target market for cards is female, eighteen to forty years of age.
- ☐ Play at the toy store.
- ☐ Listen to the radio and go to the movies (even observe popular celebrities).
- ☐ Talk to friends and family about feelings and values important to them.
- ☐ Go to the National Stationery Show in New York City.

Directories and magazines listing greeting card companies:
- ☐ *Artist's Market.*
- ☐ *Gift Reporter.*
- ☐ *Greetings Magazine.*
- ☐ *Giftware Business.*

Freelance skills needed by greeting card companies:
- ☐ Drawing and painting abilities.
- ☐ Color and design sense.
- ☐ A wide variety of style and technique: realistic, cartoon, cute or whimsical illustration, flat graphics, hand lettering, type design, airbrush, collage, photography, and three-dimensional work.
- ☐ Knowledge of finishes such as gold leaf, die cuts, and embossing.

CHAPTER 10
WHAT SHOULD YOU KNOW ABOUT ART AND DESIGN STUDIOS?

ART VS. DESIGN STUDIO

Q. *What is the difference between an art studio and a design studio?*

A. An art studio generates just that—art, usually in the form of illustration. It's not written in stone, but designers generally aren't illustrators and illustrators generally aren't designers.

A design studio concentrates on visual communications, which might utilize both illustration and photography. The design studio conceptualizes a piece, designs it, then buys the art or photography elsewhere, if necessary.

CONCEPTUALIZE

Q. *Many design studios like to see the way you "conceptualize." What does this mean in terms of what I should show them?*

A. "Conceptualizing" is the vision to see—and show—a sparkling diamond in chunks of raw coal. Most likely, you'll be showing thumbnails or roughs. Maybe it will be the complete transition of a particular assignment, from the germ of an idea through the initial thumbnails, rough sketches, comprehensive layouts, and printed piece.

SKILLS NEEDED

Q. *What freelance skills are needed by a design studio? By an art studio?*

A. In general, speed, intelligence, technical skill, and a unique perspective combined with a fresh approach. Both design and art studios will demand strong layout capabilities, good marker rendering, and excellent production skills.

Art studios will look for finished, high-quality illustration skills, welcoming a range of style and technique. They may be seeking realistic, cartoon, cute or whimsical illustration, flat graphics, hand lettering, type design, airbrush, collage, photography, or three-dimensional work—whatever gets the job done.

SPECIALIZED STUDIOS?

Q. *Do design studios specialize in certain types of work?*

A. Some do, while other studios are known for their versatility. Whether they specialize or not may actually depend on their clients' needs and demands.

Marjorie Spiegelman is president of Spiegelman Design Associates of San Francisco. In an article for *Graphic Arts Monthly,* she states, "Graphic Designers work on various scales, from letterheads and business cards to enormous, architectural three-dimensional graphics, and everything in between. We design marketing brochures, corporate identities, packaging—virtually anything that involves visual communication.

"Some designers specialize by product (annual reports); others by method (desktop publishing). Others are most remarkable for a certain style (Peter Max in the 1960s). Our design firm's specialty is neither a style nor particular product, but the way we solve problems."

LABELING YOURSELF

Q. *How do you present yourself as a designer?*

A. Design consultant David Goodman advises to first sell yourself. This begins with making the other person comfortable.

Next, observe closely and listen carefully. Talk less, listen more. When asked, "What do you do?" answer with a layered response: "I'm a graphic designer. I design (such-and-such) for companies like (so-and-so)." The key is to make meaningful contact. Remember: you are not selling anything at a first meeting; rather, you are attempting to make a good impression and generate interest.

Now, according to Goodman, comes the moment of truth: the exchange of business cards (the design of which, Goodman maintains, says more about you than the words printed on it).

TAPPING YOUR POTENTIAL

"For the first nineteen years of my life," designer/illustrator Mike Quon says, "my parents tried to convince me that I was a dentist or a doctor. Most of my education time was spent at chemistry, physics, and other sciences. I feel I got a late start; while the other kids were in art classes, I was in science courses."

Quon attended UCLA and the Art Center in Los Angeles, majoring in design and advertising (with a focus on illustration). Following school, Quon quickly learned he had a gift for snagging clients. He opened the phone book and discovered a large food services corporation in his neighborhood. He phoned, arranged a portfolio review, and came away with a large assignment. "I couldn't believe my ears—this was my first time out with this telephone calling business. I proceeded to do a press kit with insert sheets for the company, and was off and running." That first gig paid Quon $3,000 for the design and illustration, "a large amount of money in 1972 for somebody coming in right off the street."

Quon now has his own studio, the Mike Quon Design Office. Quon leads a staff of seven in turning out graphics for such clients as AT&T, American Express, Coca-Cola, and Shearson Lehman Hutton.

Quon works in a variety of areas, including identity programs, signage, and advertising illustration and design. "I am not just an illustrator, not just a designer," Quon explains. "I am involved in much more." His staff of illustrators and designers must capture not only each client's purpose but also the graphic identity of Mike Quon. "I felt I was limited, being one person and only being able to do what one person can do.

"I understand why people working purely as a designer, illustrator, or art director live longer. This triple effort has been very hard on my system. My advice is if you want to be a jack-of-all-trades, you must be willing to sacrifice a certain amount of personal time. It is extremely time consuming to do all three jobs.

"There is a lot of joy in trying other things, and if you are gifted enough to be successful in design and illustration—and have a huge energy level—I would say go for it. Most people have a difficult time doing so much in both areas. Possibly, there are people who do *more* than two areas—I'd like to know what type of vitamins they are on and where I can get them."

In marketing his skills, Quon has become adept at self-promotion. He defines the process as "trying to sell or show your work as often as possible."

His self-promotion has taken various forms over the years. "In the beginning, promotional efforts were more necessary, as time was of the essence in getting work. The assignments were more sparse when I was starting out." In contrast, his firm now handles on the average of fifteen to twenty jobs at a time, "and they always seem to be on a rush schedule."

He feels that published pieces are another form of self-promotion. "I am constantly trying to get published. In general, my methods of promotion include creating very visible projects—magazine articles, ads in directories such as *American Showcase* or the *Black Book,* and a lot of personal mailings."

Quon also awards a personalized piece of artwork to each art director with whom he works. There are over six hundred of these framed pieces around New York City alone.

"Promotion involves being something of a character and a personality," Quon admits, "which all adds up to being a very visible (and viable) talent in today's field. You must be talented and have a very good product to sell, otherwise, promotion will not deliver."

In addition to recommending artists promote their work, Quon stresses the importance of communication skills. "In its most basic form, we have to communicate with each other, and as simple as that sounds it seems to be where most of the breakdowns occur in this business. Art directors and designers don't communicate with each other. As a group, art directors and designers are not the best communicators. I sometimes question how such non-communicators have gotten into the business of communication.

"Those artists more gifted in communication seem to go a lot further along. It is important to create a nice atmosphere, and those with people skills seem to get a boost to their career that goes beyond talent. It is extremely important to get people to do what you need them to do in a timely fashion, plus it is such a tough business to begin with that working with likeable people can make a big difference."

Communication skills extend to dealing with clients in a business-like manner. "Ask as many questions as possible about final usage and how your style will work in the final printed matter. I think it's the duty of the artist to be more than a creator of images. It helps to be conscious of what the client is thinking about, the image she wants to convey, and the limits of the chosen style within what the client wants to accomplish."

Quon's parting thoughts? "This is a terribly difficult business, and you have to have all your marbles in place to get some sort of success. I make a very good living. I have received a lot of recognition and been in many shows. I've won a lot of awards, reached new plateaus, and created a nice company that does a large amount of business. These are all pleasurable things for me, but there is still this hunger and drive to attain and to produce *more,* to keep pushing and pushing into areas that I need to conquer.

"We must all ask ourselves: What do we want to get out of the business? What type of market do we want to create? Some of us have a need to make a big splash for some dumb reason, so I think we must remind ourselves that we got into this business to have a little fun—it can be an extremely fun-filled business."

© Mike Quon Design. Used with permission.

Mike Quon's Northwest Airlines piece is just one of over one hundred jobs generated by a series of Chinese zodiac drawings that appeared in *Upper & Lower Case.* This signature style has defined a timely visual language for Quon, dovetailing his Asian influences and Western communication skills. The Northwest ad is a prominent piece in Quon's portfolio, and he was contacted specifically for his bold approach and Asian point of view.

To sum up: It's not so much where you are on the ladder, but how you communicate where you want to be. As Goodman says, "Selling design actually has little to do with design. It has to do with people. Selling is a person-to-person activity."

LOCAL TALENT

Q. *Do design studios work primarily with local talent?*

A. For the most part, yes. Local talent will usually be preferred if freelance work is needed on a regular basis or to meet tight deadlines.

Aesthetically, I wouldn't limit myself to only regional design studios, and I wouldn't pigeonhole my business locally. Obviously, if you're just starting out, it makes more sense to work one-on-one with local studios, but certainly keep your eyes peeled beyond your city limits. Once you've established yourself, it will be easier to go national.

BEST INTRODUCTION

Q. *What's the best way of introducing myself, sending samples or showing my portfolio?*

A. Think of your introduction as a one-two punch. First, grab their attention with an eye-catching mailer. These initial samples get you in the door. Now, show that fabulous portfolio and display your effective communication skills.

What if you get a positive response to your brochure, but can't appear in person? Send a slide portfolio! Prepare one sleeve of no more than twenty 35mm slides (label each slide and the sleeve, plus enclose a self-addressed, postage-paid envelope for a safe return). This is easy for you, and also quite convenient for the busy art director.

Include recent tearsheets, if you have them. If not, slides alone can be very effective. Be sure to follow the package with a phone call (or enclose a self-addressed, stamped reply card) confirming receipt of your work. Try to set up appointments to meet all those nice folks who simply adore your work.

A contact may tell you that they don't require freelance help right now, and don't know when they might. Don't be discouraged. Remember those three cardinal virtues: Be polite, be persistent, be positive. Say something like, "I do understand, but I would greatly appreciate the opportunity. If I could show you my work, you can keep me in mind should anything come up."

Emphasize that you'd truly enjoy meeting them, and ask for just a moment of their time. If you still strike out, wait for another inning; try again at a later date.

BREAKING IN

Q. *What's the easiest way to break into this market?*

A. In a nutshell: If you are new in town or just starting out, work on staff for a few years. Get some actual experience at a studio before attempting to go out on your own. Learn the way a studio operates, get an idea of the type of projects design studios handle. Establish a network of contacts and a body of skills. Join organizations pertaining to the field, then freelance.

Dan Johnson, president of Art Direction, in Dayton, Ohio, says, "This is not the right question, *because there is no easy way.* What is the *best* way? A lot of hard work. There's no substitute for knocking on doors, sending mailers, making telephone calls, and being very persistent (within reason). You have to be there when the work is there, you cannot create the work. There has to be a need, and you have to fill this need.

"There are always several people who can do that, besides yourself. So you have to be in front of the contact's mind, or you have to be there at the right time. Now factor in talent, speed, and competitive pricing; these are some of the best ways to break into this market."

STUDIO STYLE

Q. *How do you research the style preferred by a design studio?*

A. A good studio won't have one style, or use only one kind of illustration. The type of illustration needed is based on the client's needs. However, you may be asked to generate imagery with a certain "look."

CHAPTER TEN CHECKLISTS

The difference between an art studio and a design studio:
☐ An art studio generates art, usually in the form of illustration.
☐ The design studio conceptualizes a piece, designs it, then buys the art or photography elsewhere, if necessary.

Freelance skills needed by these studios:
☐ Speed, intelligence, and skill.
☐ Strong layout capabilities.
☐ Good marker rendering.
☐ Excellent production skills.
☐ Drawing and painting prowess.
☐ A fine color and design sense.

Directories listing design studios:
☐ Consult the chamber of commerce and Better Business Bureau.
☐ Try your regional Business-to-Business Yellow Pages.
☐ Check the members' directory of your town's ad club.
☐ *Membership Directory of the American Institute of Graphic Arts.*
☐ *Design Firm Directory.*
☐ *L.A. Workbook.*
☐ *Adweek Portfolio.*

Organizations to join:
☐ Graphic Artists Guild.
☐ Society of Publication Designers.
☐ American Institute of Graphic Arts (AIGA).
☐ Society of Illustrators.
☐ City and Regional Magazine Association (CRMA).
☐ Society of Photographers and Artist Representatives (SPAR).
☐ Society of Typographic Arts (STA).
☐ You local ad club.
☐ Contact local universities.

Magazines focused on design:
☐ *Print.*
☐ *HOW.*
☐ *Step-By-Step Graphics.*
☐ *Communication Arts.*
☐ *Metropolis.*
☐ *Folio.*
☐ *Confetti.*
☐ *Magazine Design & Production.*
☐ *Upper & Lower Case.*
☐ *Graphis.*
☐ *Advertising Age.*
☐ *Ad Week.*
☐ *Graphic Design Monthly.*

CHAPTER 11
HOW DO YOU SELL WORK TO SMALL BUSINESSES?

NEW VS. ESTABLISHED

Q. *Should you work with new or established businesses?*

A. As an illustrator or designer with fresh, bold ideas, it may be better to work with new businesses, but be careful—new businesses frequently fail and don't pay. Established businesses (presumably with some sort of cash flow) are a better bet, but may not grant any creative freedom. Remember, do your homework, and prior to accepting an assignment for *any* company:

- Take good notes.
- Ask incisive questions.
- Know (and be ready to discuss) your rates.
- Evaluate how the client's needs jibe with your own.
- Be up front and clear about terms.
- Don't be afraid to ask for what you really need to do the assignment. Don't be pressured into cutting the deal on the spot.
- Get written documentation at the beginning of a job (or do the paper work from your end).
- If need be, minimize risk by asking for payments at various points of completion.
- Approach all negotiations with open eyes and mind.
- Remember that negotiation is a learning process.

TYPES OF WORK NEEDED

Q. *What type of freelance help do small businesses need?*

A. Many folks consider working with small businesses to be bargain basement, low-budget, "clip art"-type grunt work; we can be more creative and industrious than that, can't we?

It could be creating a logo for a business card or drawing the illustration for an upcoming newspaper ad. You may design and paint bold interior graphics or use that logo for the shop's exterior sign. Perhaps while adapting both logo and ad illustration for a direct mailer, you'll be working up a new drawing for a postcard reminder at the same time.

How about interior signage? Pricing and sales change regularly and the store owner's handlettering just won't cut it. Besides, he loves your funny characters from the ad and wants you to incorporate them into the store displays!

VARIETY OF SMALL BUSINESSES

Q. *What type of small businesses need freelance artwork?*

A. Small businesses are not just the little hardware store down the street. There are a lot of independent companies out there that are truly businesses and are quite small. But small businesses can also mean those businesses down the street.

All small businesses have some sort of visual needs, from simple stationery or business cards to advertising, promotion, display, and signage. Perhaps you've noticed a business that doesn't have a graphic profile—that might be a good place to start. Maybe it never crossed their mind to use print vehicles to get their message across.

The wise small-business person knows that good graphics sell products. A storeowner may carefully watch the advertising budget, but is conscious of the fact that successful businesses probably got that way through advertising.

If the business is on a limited budget, the owner isn't working with an agency. He or she probably has no art background and will certainly not have your design sense or technical expertise. Smart enough to know what's needed, but with no idea how to get it together, the small-business person turns to you for quality, affordable graphics.

A small shop owner's graphics may not justify employing an agency, but those same advertising agencies in town want you. As local

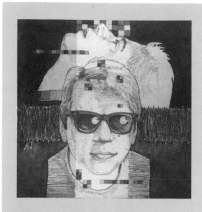

ALWAYS AIM HIGHER

In 1977, Fred Carlson received a BFA in graphic design (with university honors) from Carnegie Mellon University in Pittsburgh, Pennsylvania.

"I grew up in a small town in New England," Carlson tells us, "and just drew and painted for fun. I was guided by an interesting art teacher who had a print-making background, which fueled my interest in doing illustration. I like to see my work in print and see multiple reproductions of it, as opposed to a one-of-a-kind painting, where the painting stands on its own merit."

After four years of design education, Carlson realized that he wanted to focus more on illustration, so while he acquired his major, he also took a lot of drawing and painting courses. "I realized that graphic designers had to rely so much on suppliers, typesetters, stat houses, photographers, illustrators, keyline artists, and printers," he says. "You were at the center of a bunch of spokes. If you couldn't control the ebb and flow of all those spokes, then you'd be a nervous wreck, and I frankly couldn't see how anybody made money doing it."

Wanting to be in charge of his own finished images and be responsible for finished solutions, Carlson took a job with Pitt Studios. "My first assignments for the studio were for Westinghouse Corporation," he recalls. "Ketchum Advertising (Westinghouse's advertising agency) farmed their art needs to our studio. I remember doing many marker comps (as well as finished art) for campaigns they would pitch to their clients.

"Ketchum would assign the work to our sales reps, who would bring it in and chan-nel it through our art director to the various illustrators. It would then go back out through that chain of command, back to the art director and back to the rep. The rep would present it to Ketchum, and they would present the work to Westinghouse.

"I began to get freelance work when I was still on staff, mostly local, regional and city magazine assignments—the budgets were not large enough to warrant any studio concerns over me doing the work. As you move through your field you stay in contact with your classmates, and a lot of them become designers and art directors. You can get assignments from those people. They have a need for what you do and remember you as either a dependable person or a schnook.

"After three years of working at the studio, my first major freelance assignment arrived in the form of a corporate calendar for Westinghouse. The contact was made through a former sales rep of the studio, now servicing Westinghouse accounts. He wanted to know if I would be interested in doing six pieces for this major calendar series, a buy-out for $4,800, with the originals going to Westinghouse's corporate collection.

"At that point I realized I could not keep working for the studio because Westinghouse was one of their clients, so when I made the commitment to do this calendar series, I knew I would be leaving anyway."

Working on staff for three years enabled Carlson to understand the business and realize his potential, to appreciate deadlines, and test his abilities under stress. "I became a better illustrator because of all these demands on me in the studio," Carlson points out.

"I got used to long hours working during the day and then freelancing at night—it was like being in physical training for a long-distance race. You have to prepare yourself—you have to work out and extend yourself. If you've never encountered those demands before—like you're running a marathon for the first time—then you're going to drop out."

How does Carlson go the distance to maintain a thriving business? "I buy national space in creative directories," he explains. "I order reprints of those trade ads, as well as getting my own promotional pieces printed up locally, then I use direct mail to get them out.

"I try to do two to four mailings a year, based on my mailing list. It gets into some sizable postage, but it's worth it—it beats taking a day and going to see one or two clients personally. That costs more time and dollars to me than spending $200 on stamps and sending out eight hundred mailers.

"The promotional pieces I use are generally formatted with three to five images of whatever I feel is new and exciting *to me*. I'm at the point in my career where I need new challenges. I can always rely on my steady accounts and I'm always looking for new accounts, so I think: 'What sort of images do I want to go after this year?' I then pull out those jobs as my advertising."

What goes into a beginner's portfolio? Says Carlson, "Put in samples that relate to solving problems. The samples should not make the art buyer ask questions, they should answer questions. The buyer has a set of questions in mind: Are you dependable? Can you work with different size restrictions? Can you solve demanding compositional requirements? All these things. Your samples must be positive answers to those questions.

"Avoid mediocre or bad art. Be very critical. You have to look at your work in a very detached manner. This is extremely hard for young artists to do because you have such a personal stake in each piece. However, this isn't going to help you get jobs because the work isn't always going to relate to everybody.

"Make sure every piece in your portfolio is as good as it can be—no half-way accomplished tasks. Have samples that solve a wide range of problems with stylistic consistency as well as mental latitude."

Carlson says a beginner should have an image in mind of what he or she would like to be in ten years, "then never waver from that."

Carlson also advises beginners to maintain quality in all jobs. "Always work towards the next plateau and dedicate 100 percent of your ability to every job. Don't compromise—encourage quality in yourself and your clients. Push yourself to go beyond what the assignment requires.

"Don't be in it for the money—know that you're working for your personal survival fund and that there's always another job coming down! Think of yourself as a business, and you're trying to enhance, mar-

© Fred Carlson. Used with permission.

Fred Carlson says, "I've discovered that the types of jobs you get—from design firms, agencies, corporations, small businesses, books, magazines, your own promotional thing—are all going to demand different things from you."

A 1984 brochure through McCullough Communications found Carlson illustrating five pertinent subjects for the Ferguson Foundation, including this example relating to research into athletic injuries and bone cancer in children. Terms on this job included a buyout of the original art.

ket, sell, and promote that business."

In closing, Carlson advises one and all to keep their relationships up with other illustrators, designers, and art buyers. "Don't feel too competitive with other illustrators, because everybody does different kinds of work. Nobody can sit there and copy somebody else, so everyone has something different to sell.

"If you have good personal relationships with a number of illustrators, you can share trade news or general gossip about what's new and what's moving around in your market. I find this very important. I don't like to have secrets from other illustrators. It's not helpful for illustrators to fight about things. It's such a tough way to make a living anyway. You have to share as much information as possible."

talent you're able to meet tight deadlines and will understand the needs of your buying community. Your hometown sensibilities are a big plus on regional accounts.

The same thing applies for neighborhood newsletters, town newspapers, and city or regional magazines. Often these publications will only work with regional talent because these artists are neighbors who understand the issues and the current events that affect the local population.

A shoe store employs you to do customer caricatures as a buyer's incentive. One happy customer, a restaurant manager, loves the gimmick and asks you to roam his bistro weekend evenings. A patron enjoys your work so much she hires you to do a party and commissions a birthday portrait as well.

The public television station, the university, a deli, even your dentist—any small or local business with print demands, and that's every business that advertises or generates correspondence, can use freelance help.

These small businesses are only your first stops. Good assignments are where you find them, and the path to a wealth of opportunities begins in your own backyard.

INTRODUCING YOURSELF

Q. *How do you find out if a local business needs freelance artwork?*

A. The best way is to simply introduce yourself by publicizing your services. Yes, marketing and self-promotion again! Your local program is important. You have the decided advantage and incentive of knowing the home turf, so take a direct and aggressive approach.

"Aggressive" does not mean obnoxious or overbearing; it means a keen and concerted effort. Mail your brochure and follow up with a phone call about a week later. You're literally in the neighborhood, so don't let the contact go cold. Ask for the store owner or manager.

Introduce yourself, make sure the brochure arrived, and tell this person you'll be making the rounds on a certain day, at a certain time. Ask if it would be okay to drop in and schmooze, perhaps show some samples, too.

You're obviously after an affirmative re-

sponse, but even if there's no job and you get a positive reaction, go to talk and gather information. Bring your portfolio, but forget the big sales pitch. Lay the groundwork for your continued promotion. Chances are, when there is a need, they'll remember that person with the pleasant smile and beautiful art work.

If they ask not to be bothered, believe them. These are busy people, so don't pester. Say, "Perhaps another time, if this is inconvenient?" or "May I keep you on my mailing list and call again for a future appointment?"

Chatting up the main avenue of the business district will probably take no more time than your usual stroll when shopping; it could be the most lucrative window shopping you ever do.

FINDING NEW BUSINESSES

Q. *How do you find out when a new business is about to open?*

A. New construction or reconstruction is an obvious tip-off. Keep your eyes open, wade through the dust, and make inquiries.

The chamber of commerce should be able to supply you with a list of new businesses in your area. Business trade publications in most markets publish corporate announcements; business magazines on a local level like to welcome new businesses to that market. New businesses about to open often issue press releases to the local media; watch for that. Check the newspaper for grand opening announcements or lists of incorporations.

WHOM TO CALL

Q. *Whom do you contact at a small business?*

A. The store owner or manager is your best bet. A sales clerk, while receptive, won't have the authority to commission your work. However, as the sales staff has the ear of the store-owner, staffers could be allies to your cause. If the boss is presently unavailable, begin with the clerk and make a date to return.

SAMPLES

Q. *What type of samples should you show to a small-business person?*

A. The small-business person is interested in how you can help the store, so your samples will have to generally relate to the business environment.

Illustrator Fred Carlson says, "I've found that, while some clients buy style and some markets buy subject matter, they're probably more subject matter-oriented. Small businesses buy subject matter that relates to what they're doing. The visual should be easy to reproduce. You can't present an extremely complicated image with a lot of halftone variations to a small-business owner; they're not going to spend the money to print those kinds of things.

"Small businesses have fairly simple print needs and relatively small budgets for print, so show artwork that fits in with lower budgets."

ART DIRECTING YOURSELF

Q. *Small businesses generally don't have an art director. Does this mean you will have to not only create the artwork but also get it printed?*

A. You might, but don't pass up an opportunity to work with a printer because "it just means more work (grumble, grumble)." If you're worried about the finished product or merely want to further your graphics education, it's to your advantage to see the job through to the end. Why not factor added responsibilities into your bid and have a fun learning experience at the same time?

Fred Carlson says, "You may very well be asked, 'You can do the drawing, but can you do the production and design, and get it printed?' This falls in your lap sometimes because the buyer isn't that sophisticated about the division of labor in the graphic arts, so they might just assume that you, as an illustrator, would know all these other things. What you should say is: 'Sure, I can do all those extra things—it will cost you, but I'm certainly willing to do it.'

"If you maintain this relationship with certain local clients, it keeps the checks coming. The more you specialize, the less chance of a relationship with a small business. They're going to have the most basic needs, and if you can service those basic needs, you're going to do all right."

LOCALS PREFERRED?

Q. *Are small businesses open to freelancers who don't live nearby?*

A. Realistically, you don't have to live down the block from the store to service a small business account. However, if your distance from any theater of operation inhibits the job hunt or delays completion of an assignment, location can be a liability.

WORKING THROUGH DESIGN STUDIOS

Q. *Several local businesses assign their work to design studios. Does this mean they wouldn't need any freelance help?*

A. Not necessarily. A design studio will probably handle all aspects of a particular job. This shouldn't discourage you from showing your work to a small-business owner, as the studio usually farms out the illustration end of the project. The owner may encourage the studio to use you. Find out about that same design studio and show your work or mail samples. It will certainly help your chances. If the studio doesn't have an exclusive arrangement with the store, you may want to approach the owner regarding other graphic needs around the establishment.

SOURCES OF NAMES

Q. *Are there sources other than the Yellow Pages for names of local businesses?*

A. The chamber of commerce and the Better Business Bureau are your best bets here—and join your local art directors club.

CHAPTER ELEVEN
CHECKLISTS

When working with new or established businesses:

- ☐ Take good notes.
- ☐ Ask incisive questions.
- ☐ Know (and be ready to discuss) your rates.
- ☐ Evaluate how the client's needs jibe with your own.
- ☐ Be up front and clear about terms.
- ☐ Don't be afraid to ask for what you really need to do the assignment—and don't be pressured into cutting the deal on the spot.
- ☐ Get written documentation at the beginning of a job (or do the paper work from your end).
- ☐ If need be, minimize risk by asking for payments at various points of completion.
- ☐ Approach all negotiations with open eyes and mind.
- ☐ Remember that negotiation is a learning process.

The type of freelance help small businesses need:

- ☐ Creating a logo for a business card.
- ☐ Drawing the illustration for an upcoming newspaper ad.
- ☐ Designing and painting interior graphics or a logo for an exterior sign.
- ☐ Working on a direct mailer.
- ☐ Illustrating a postcard reminder.
- ☐ Creating interior signage.

The types of small businesses that need freelance artwork:

- ☐ Local advertising agencies.
- ☐ Neighborhood newsletters, town newspapers.
- ☐ City or regional magazines.
- ☐ A shoe store, a restaurant, the public television station, the university, a deli, your dentist—any small or local business with print demands.

To find out if a local business needs freelance artwork:

- ☐ Publicize your services.
- ☐ Mail your brochure and follow with a phone call about a week later; ask for the store owner or manager.
- ☐ Introduce yourself; ask for an appointment.
- ☐ Bring your portfolio; lay the groundwork for your continued promotion.

To find out when a new business is about to open:

- ☐ Watch for new construction or reconstruction.
- ☐ Ask the chamber of commerce.
- ☐ Consult business trade publications for corporate announcements.
- ☐ Read local business magazines.
- ☐ Look for press releases to the local media.
- ☐ Check the newspaper for grand opening announcements or lists of incorporations.

INDEX

Improve your skills, learn a new technique, with these additional books from North Light

Graphics/Business of Art

Airbrush Artist's Library (6 in series) $12.95 (cloth)
Airbrush Techniques Workbooks (8 in series) $9.95 each
Airbrushing the Human Form, by Andy Charlesworth $19.95 (cloth)
Artist's Friendly Legal Guide, by Floyd Conner, Peter Karlan, Jean Perwin & David M. Spatt $18.95 (paper)
Artist's Market: Where & How to Sell Your Graphic Art (Annual Directory) $19.95 (cloth)
Basic Desktop Design & Layout, by Collier & Cotton $27.95 (cloth)
Basic Graphic Design & Paste-Up, by Jack Warren $13.95 (paper)
Business & Legal Forms for Graphic Designers, by Tad Crawford $19.95 (paper)
Business and Legal Forms for Illustrators, by Tad Crawford $15.95
CLICK: The Brightest in Computer-Generated Design and Illustration $39.95 (cloth)
COLORWORKS: The Designer's Ultimate Guide to Working with Color, by Dale Russell (5 in series) $24.95 ea.
Color Harmony: A Guide to Creative Color Combinations, by Hideaki Chijiiwa $15.95 (paper)
Complete Airbrush & Photoretouching Manual, by Peter Owen & John Sutcliffe $24.95 (cloth)
The Complete Book of Caricature, by Bob Staake $18.95
The Complete Guide to Greeting Card Design & Illustration, by Eva Szela $27.95 (cloth)
Creating Dynamic Roughs, by Alan Swann $27.95 (cloth)
Creative Director's Sourcebook, by Nick Souter and Stuart Neuman $89.00 (cloth)
Creative Typography, by Marion March $27.95 (cloth)
Design Rendering Techniques, by Dick Powell $29.95 (cloth)
The Designer's Commonsense Business Book, by Barbara Ganim $22.95 (paper)
Designing with Color, by Roy Osborne $26.95 (cloth)
Dynamic Airbrush, by David Miller & James Effler $29.95 (cloth)
Fantasy Art, by Bruce Robertson $24.95 (cloth)
Fashion Illustration Workbooks (4 in series) $8.95 each
59 More Studio Secrets, by Susan Davis $29.95 (cloth)
47 Printing Headaches (and How To Avoid Them), by Linda S. Sanders $24.95 (paper)
Getting It Printed, by Beach, Shepro & Russon $29.50 (paper)
Getting Started as a Freelance Illustrator or Designer, by Michael Fleischman $16.95 (paper)
Getting Started in Computer Graphics, by Gary Olsen $27.95 (paper)
Getting the Max from Your Graphics Computer, by Lisa Walker & Steve Blount $27.95 (paper)
The Graphic Artist's Guide to Marketing & Self-Promotion, by Sally Prince Davis $19.95 (paper)

The Graphic Designer's Basic Guide to the Macintosh, by Meyerowitz and Sanchez $19.95 (paper)
Graphic Idea Notebook, by Jan V. White $19.95 (paper)
Graphics Handbook, by Howard Munce $14.95 (paper)
Handbook of Pricing & Ethical Guidelines, 7th edition, by The Graphic Artist's Guild $22.95 (paper)
Homage to the Alphabet: Typeface Sourcebook, $39.95 (cloth)
HOT AIR: An Explosive Collection of Top Airbrush Illustration, $39.95 (cloth)
How to Check and Correct Color Proofs, by David Bann $27.95 (cloth)
How to Design Trademarks & Logos, by Murphy & Row $19.95 (paper)
How to Draw & Sell Cartoons, by Ross Thomson & Bill Hewison $18.95 (cloth)
How to Draw & Sell Comic Strips, by Alan McKenzie $18.95 (cloth)
How to Draw Charts & Diagrams, by Bruce Robertson $24.95 (cloth)
How to Find and Work with an Illustrator, by Martin Colyer $24.95 (cloth)
How to Understand & Use Design & Layout, by Alan Swann $19.95 (paper)
How to Understand & Use Grids, by Alan Swann $27.95 (cloth)
How to Write and Illustrate Children's Books, edited by Treld Pelkey Bicknell and Felicity Trotman, $22.50 (cloth)
International Logotypes 2, edited by Yasaburo Kuwayama $24.95 (paper)
Label Design 2, by Walker and Blount $49.95 (cloth)
Legal Guide for the Visual Artist, Revised Edition by Tad Crawford $18.95 (paper)
Letterhead & Logo Designs: Creating the Corporate Image $49.95 (cloth)
Licensing Art & Design, by Caryn Leland $12.95 (paper)
Living by Your Brush Alone, by Edna Wagner Piersol $16.95 (paper)
Make It Legal, by Lee Wilson $18.95 (paper)
Making Your Computer a Design & Business Partner, by Walker and Blount $27.95 (paper)
Marker Rendering Techniques, by Dick Powell & Patricia Monahan $32.95 (cloth)
Marker Techniques Workbooks (8 in series) $9.95 each
North Light Dictionary of Art Terms, by Margy Lee Elspass $12.95 (paper)
Papers for Printing, by Mark Beach & Ken Russon $39.50 (paper)
Preparing Your Design for Print, by Lynn John $27.95 (cloth)
Presentation Techniques for the Graphic Artist, by Jenny Mulherin $24.95 (cloth)
Primo Angeli: Designs for Marketing, $19.95 (paper)
Print Production Handbook, by David Bann $16.95 (cloth)
Print's Best Corporate Publications $34.95 (cloth)

Product Design: New & Notable, by Christie Thomas & the editors of *International Design* Magazine $49.95 (cloth)

The Professional Designer's Guide to Marketing Your Work, by Mary Yeung $29.95

Ready to Use Layouts for Desktop Design, by Chris Prior $27.95 (cloth)

Type & Color: A Handbook of Creative Combinations, by Cook and Fleury $34.95 (cloth)

Type: Design, Color, Character & Use, by Michael Beaumont $19.95 (paper)

Type Recipes, by Gregory Wolfe $19.95 (paper)

Typewise, written & designed by Kit Hinrichs with Delphine Hirasuna $39.95

The Ultimate Portfolio, by Martha Metzdorf $32.95

Using Type Right, by Philip Brady $18.95 (paper)

Art & Activity Books For Kids

Draw!, by Kim Solga $11.95
Paint!, by Kim Solga $11.95
Make Prints!, by Kim Solga $11.95
Make Gifts!, by Kim Solga $11.95

Watercolor

Basic Watercolor Techniques, edited by Greg Albert & Rachel Wolf $14.95 (paper)

Big Brush Watercolor, by Ron Ranson $22.95 (cloth)

Buildings in Watercolor, by Richard S. Taylor $24.95 (paper)

Chinese Watercolor Painting: The Four Seasons, by Leslie Tseng-Tseng Yu $24.95 (paper)

The Complete Watercolor Book, by Wendon Blake $29.95 (cloth)

Fill Your Watercolors with Light and Color, by Roland Roycraft $27.95 (cloth)

Flower Painting, by Paul Riley $27.95 (cloth)

Getting Started in Watercolor, by John Blockley $19.95 (paper)

How to Make Watercolor Work for You, by Frank Nofer $27.95 (cloth)

Jan Kunz Watercolor Techniques Workbook 1: Painting the Still Life, by Jan Kunz $12.95 (paper)

Jan Kunz Watercolor Techniques Workbook 2: Painting Children's Portraits, by Jan Kunz $12.95 (paper)

The New Spirit of Watercolor, by Mike Ward $21.95 (paper)

Painting Nature's Details in Watercolor, by Cathy Johnson $21.95 (paper)

Painting Watercolor Portraits That Glow, by Jan Kunz $27.95 (cloth)

Splash I, edited by Greg Albert & Rachel Wolf $29.95

Starting with Watercolor, by Rowland Hilder $24.95 (cloth)

Tony Couch Watercolor Techniques, by Tony Couch $14.95 (paper)

Watercolor Impressionists, edited by Ron Ranson $45.00 (cloth)

Watercolor Painter's Solution Book, by Angela Gair $19.95 (paper)

Watercolor Painter's Pocket Palette, edited by Moira Clinch $15.95 (cloth)

Watercolor: Painting Smart, by Al Stine $27.95 (cloth)

Watercolor — The Creative Experience, by Barbara Nechis $16.95 (paper)

Watercolor Tricks & Techniques, by Cathy Johnson $24.95 (cloth)

Watercolor Workbook, by Bud Biggs & Lois Marshall $19.95 (paper)

Watercolor: You Can Do It!, by Tony Couch $26.95 (cloth)

Webb on Watercolor, by Frank Webb $29.95 (cloth)

The Wilcox Guide to the Best Watercolor Paints, by Michael Wilcox $24.95 (paper)

Mixed Media

The Art of Scratchboard, by Cecile Curtis $23.95 (cloth)

The Artist's Complete Health & Safety Guide, by Monona Rossol $16.95 (paper)

Basic Drawing Techniques, edited by Greg Albert & Rachel Wolf $14.95 (paper)

Blue and Yellow Don't Make Green, by Michael Wilcox $24.95 (cloth)

Bodyworks: A Visual Guide to Drawing the Figure, by Marbury Hill Brown $24.95 (cloth)

Business & Legal Forms for Fine Artists, by Tad Crawford $12.95 (paper)

Calligraphy Workbooks (4 in series) $7.95 each

Capturing Light & Color with Pastel, by Doug Dawson $27.95 (cloth)

Colored Pencil Drawing Techniques, by Iain Hutton-Jamieson $24.95 (cloth)

The Complete Acrylic Painting Book, by Wendon Blake $29.95 (cloth)

The Complete Guide to Screenprinting, by Brad Faine $24.95 (cloth)

Complete Guide to Fashion Illustration, by Colin Barnes $32.95 (cloth)

The Creative Artist, by Nita Leland $27.95 (cloth)

Creative Basketmaking, by Lois Walpole $24.95 (cloth)

Creative Painting with Pastel, by Carole Katchen $27.95 (cloth)

Decorative Painting for Children's Rooms, by Rosie Fisher $29.95 (cloth)

The Dough Book, by Toni Bergli Joner $19.95 (cloth)

Drawing & Painting Animals, by Cecile Curtis $26.95 (cloth)

Drawing Workbooks (4 in series) $8.95 each

Dynamic Color Drawing, by Judy Martin $26.95 (cloth)

Exploring Color, by Nita Leland $22.95 (paper)

Festive Folding, by Paul Jackson $22.95 (cloth)

Fine Artist's Guide to Showing & Selling Your Work, by Sally Price Davis $17.95 (paper)

The Figure, edited by Walt Reed $16.95 (paper)
Getting Started in Drawing, by Wendon Blake $24.95
The Half Hour Painter, by Alwyn Crawshaw $19.95 (paper)
Handtinting Photographs, by Martin and Colbeck $28.95 (cloth)
How to Paint Living Portraits, by Roberta Carter Clark $27.95 (cloth)
How to Succeed As An Artist In Your Hometown, by Stewart P. Biehl $24.95 (paper)
Introduction to Batik, by Griffin & Holmes $9.95 (paper)
Keys to Drawing, by Bert Dodson $19.95 (paper)
Light: How to See It, How to Paint It, by Lucy Willis $19.95 (paper)
Make Your Own Picture Frames, by Jenny Rodwell $12.95 (paper)
Master Strokes, by Jennifer Bennell $24.95 (cloth)
The North Light Handbook of Artist's Materials, by Ian Hebblewhite $24.95 (cloth)
The North Light Illustrated Book of Painting Techniques, by Elizabeth Tate $27.95 (cloth)
Oil Painting: Develop Your Natural Ability, by Charles Sovek $27.95
Oil Painting: A Direct Approach, by Joyce Pike $26.95 (cloth)
Painting Floral Still Lifes, by Joyce Pike $19.95 (paper)
Painting Landscapes in Oils, by Mary Anna Goetz $27.95 (cloth)

Painting More Than the Eye Can See, by Robert Wade $29.95 (cloth)
Painting Seascapes in Sharp Focus, by Lin Seslar $21.95 (paper)
Painting the Beauty of Flowers with Oils, by Pat Moran $27.95 (cloth)
Painting with Acrylics, by Jenny Rodwell $19.95 (paper)
Painting with Oils, by Patricia Monahan $19.95 (cloth)
Pastel Painting Techniques, by Guy Roddon $19.95 (paper)
The Pencil, by Paul Calle $17.95 (paper)
Perspective Without Pain Workbooks (4 in series) $9.95 each
Photographing Your Artwork, by Russell Hart $16.95 (paper)
Realistic Figure Drawing, by Joseph Sheppard $19.95 (paper)

To order directly from the publisher, include $3.00 postage and handling for one book, $1.00 for each additional book. Allow 30 days for delivery.
North Light Books
1507 Dana Avenue, Cincinnati, Ohio 45207
Credit card orders
Call TOLL-FREE
1-800-289-0963
Prices subject to change without notice.